Learn Italian with Starter Stories

HypLern Interlinear Project
www.hyplern.com

First edition: 2025, July

Author: Various
Translation: Kees van den End
Foreword: Camilo Andrés Bonilla Carvajal PhD

ISBN: 978-1-988830-91-9

kees@hyplern.com
www.hyplern.com

Learn Italian with Starter Stories

Interlinear Italian to English

Author
Various

Translation
Kees van den End

HypLern Interlinear Project
www.hyplern.com

The HypLern Method

Learning a foreign language should not mean leafing through page after page in a bilingual dictionary until one's fingertips begin to hurt. Quite the contrary, through everyday language use, friendly reading, and direct exposure to the language we can get well on our way towards mastery of the vocabulary and grammar needed to read native texts. In this manner, learners can be successful in the foreign language without too much study of grammar paradigms or rules. Indeed, Seneca expresses in his sixth epistle that "Longum iter est per praecepta, breve et efficax per exempla[1]."

The HypLern series constitutes an effort to provide a highly effective tool for experiential foreign language learning. Those who are genuinely interested in utilizing original literary works to learn a foreign language do not have to use conventional graded texts or adapted versions for novice readers. The former only distort the actual essence of literary works, while the latter are highly reduced in vocabulary and relevant content. This collection aims to bring the lively experience of reading stories as directly told by their very authors to foreign language learners.

Most excited adult language learners will at some point seek their teachers' guidance on the process of learning to read in the foreign language rather than seeking out external opinions. However, both teachers and learners lack a general reading technique or strategy. Oftentimes, students undertake the reading task equipped with nothing more than a bilingual dictionary, a grammar book, and lots of courage. These efforts often end in frustration as the student builds mis-constructed nonsensical sentences after many hours spent on an aimless translation drill.

Consequently, we have decided to develop this series of interlinear translations intended to afford a comprehensive edition of unabridged texts. These texts are presented as they were originally written with no changes in word choice or order. As a result, we have a translated piece conveying the true meaning under every word from the original work. Our readers receive then two books in just one volume: the original version and its translation.

The reading task is no longer a laborious exercise of patiently decoding unclear and seemingly complex paragraphs. What's more, reading becomes an enjoyable and meaningful process of cultural, philosophical and linguistic learning. Independent learners can then acquire expressions and vocabulary while understanding pragmatic and socio-cultural dimensions of the target language by reading in it rather than reading about it.

Our proposal, however, does not claim to be a novelty. Interlinear translation is as old as the Spanish tongue, e.g. "glosses of [Saint] Emilianus", interlinear bibles in Old German, and of course James Hamilton's work in the 1800s. About the latter, we remind the readers, that as a revolutionary freethinker he promoted the publication of Greco-Roman classic works and further pieces in diverse languages. His effort, such as ours, sought to lighten the exhausting task of looking words up in large glossaries as an educational practice: "if there is any thing which fills reflecting men with melancholy and regret, it is the waste of mortal time, parental money, and puerile happiness, in the present method of pursuing Latin and Greek[2]".

Additionally, another influential figure in the same line of thought as Hamilton was John Locke. Locke was also the philosopher and translator of the Fabulae AEsopi in an interlinear plan. In 1600, he was already suggesting that interlinear texts, everyday communication, and use of the target language could be the most appropriate ways to achieve language learning:

> ...the true and genuine Way, and that which I would propose, not only as the easiest and best, wherein a Child might, without pains or Chiding, get a Language which others are wont to be whipt for at School six or seven Years together...[3]

---

1   "The journey is long through precepts, but brief and effective through examples". Seneca, Lucius Annaeus. (1961) Ad Lucilium Epistulae Morales, vol. I. London: W. Heinemann.

2   In: Hamilton, James (1829?) History, principles, practice and results of the Hamiltonian system, with answers to the Edinburgh and Westminster reviews; A lecture delivered at Liverpool; and instructions for the use of the books published on the system. Londres: W. Aylott and Co., 8, Pater Noster Row. p. 29.

3   In: Locke, John. (1693) Some thoughts concerning education. Londres: A. and J. Churchill. pp. 196-7.

Who can benefit from this edition?

We identify three kinds of readers, namely, those who take this work as a search tool, those who want to learn a language by reading authentic materials, and those attempting to read writers in their original language. The HypLern collection constitutes a very effective instrument for all of them.

1. For the first target audience, this edition represents a search tool to connect their mother tongue with that of the writer's. Therefore, they have the opportunity to read over an original literary work in an enriching and certain manner.
2. For the second group, reading every word or idiomatic expression in its actual context of use will yield a strong association between the form, the collocation, and the context. This will have a direct impact on long term learning of passive vocabulary, gradually building genuine reading ability in the original language. This book is an ideal companion not only to independent learners but also to those who take lessons with a teacher. At the same time, the continuous feeling of achievement produced during the process of reading original authors both stimulates and empowers the learner to study[1].
3. Finally, the third kind of reader will notice the same benefits as the previous ones. The proximity of a word and its translation in our interlinear texts is a step further from other collections, such as the Loeb Classical Library. Although their works might be considered the most famous in this genre, the presentation of texts on opposite pages hinders the immediate link between words and their semantic equivalence in our native tongue (or one we have a strong mastery of).

---

1 Some further ways of using the present work include:

1. As you progress through the stories, focus less on the lower line (the English translation). Instead, try to read through the upper line, staying in the foreign language as long as possible.
2. Even if you find glosses or explanatory footnotes about the mechanics of the language, you should make your own hypotheses on word formation and syntactical functions in a sentence. Feel confident about inferring your own language rules and test them progressively. You can also take notes concerning those idiomatic expressions or special language usage that calls your attention for later study.
3. As soon as you finish each text, check the reading in the original version (with no interlinear or parallel translation). This will fulfil the main goal of this

collection: bridging the gap between readers and original literary works, training them to read directly and independently.

Why interlinear?

Conventionally speaking, tiresome reading in tricky and exhausting circumstances has been the common definition of learning by texts. This collection offers a friendly reading format where the language is not a stumbling block anymore. Contrastively, our collection presents a language as a vehicle through which readers can attain and understand their authors' written ideas.

While learning to read, most people are urged to use the dictionary and distinguish words from multiple entries. We help readers skip this step by providing the proper translation based on the surrounding context. In so doing, readers have the chance to invest energy and time in understanding the text and learning vocabulary; they read quickly and easily like a skilled horseman cantering through a book.

Thereby we stress the fact that our proposal is not new at all. Others have tried the same before, coming up with evident and substantial outcomes. Certainly, we are not pioneers in designing interlinear texts. Nonetheless, we are nowadays the only, and doubtless, the best, in providing you with interlinear foreign language texts.

Handling instructions

Using this book is very easy. Each text should be read at least three times in order to explore the whole potential of the method. The first phase is devoted to comparing words in the foreign language to those in the mother tongue. This is to say, the upper line is contrasted to the lower line as the following example shows:

Egli	le	domandò	dove	andava.
He	her	asked	where	(she) went

The second phase of reading focuses on capturing the meaning and sense of the original text. As readers gain practice with the method, they should be able to focus on the target language without getting distracted by the translation. New users of the method, however, may find it helpful to cover the translated lines with a piece of paper as illustrated in the image below. Subsequently, they try to understand the meaning of every word, phrase, and entire sentences in the target language itself, drawing on the translation only when necessary. In this phase, the reader should resist the temptation to look at the translation for every word. In doing so, they will find that they are able to understand a good portion of the text by reading directly in the target language, without the crutch of the translation. This is the skill we are looking to train: the ability to read and understand native materials and enjoy them as native speakers do, that being, directly in the original language.

Egli le domandò dove andava.
He her asked

In the final phase, readers will be able to understand the meaning of the text when reading it without additional help. There may be some less common words and phrases which have not cemented themselves yet in the reader's brain, but the majority of the story should not pose any problems. If desired, the reader can use an SRS or some other memorization method to learning these straggling words.

Egli le domandò dove andava.

Above all, readers will not have to look every word up in a dictionary to read a text in the foreign language. This otherwise wasted time will be spent concentrating on their principal interest. These new readers will tackle authentic texts while learning their vocabulary and expressions to use in further communicative (written or oral) situations. This book is just one work from an overall series with the same purpose. It really helps those who are afraid of having "poor vocabulary" to feel confident about reading directly in the language. To all of them and to all of you, welcome to the amazing experience of living a foreign language!

Additional tools

Check out shop.hyplern.com or contact us at info@hyplern.com for free mp3s (if available) and free empty (untranslated) versions of the eBooks that we have on offer.

For some of the older eBooks and paperbacks we have Windows, iOS and Android apps available that, next to the interlinear format, allow for a pop-up format, where hovering over a word or clicking on it gives you its meaning. The apps also have any mp3s, if available, and integrated vocabulary practice.

Visit the site hyplern.com for the same functionality online. This is where we will be working non-stop to make all our material available in multiple formats, including audio where available, and vocabulary practice.

Table of Contents

Cappuccetto Rosso

Cappuccetto Rosso
Little hood Red
Little Red Riding Hood

C'era una volta in un villaggio una bambina, la
There was one time in a village a child the
{feminine}

più carina che si potesse mai vedere. La sua
most dear that oneself could ever see The -her-

mamma n'era matta, e la sua nonna
mamma for her was crazy and -the- her grandmother
was very fond of her

anche di più.
even -of- more

Quella buona donna di sua madre le aveva fatto
That good woman of her mother her had made

fare un cappuccetto rosso, il quale le tornava
make a little cap red -the- which her turned
(became)

così bene a viso, che la chiamavano
so well to (the) face that her (they) called

dappertutto Cappuccetto Rosso.
everywhere Little hood Red

Un giorno sua madre, avendo cavate di forno
One day her mother having obtained from (the) oven

alcune stiacciate, le disse:
some focacio's her said
(unleavened breads)

"Va' un po' a vedere come sta la tua nonna,
Go a bit to see how is -the- your grandmother

perché mi hanno detto che era un po'
because me (they) have said that (she) was a bit

incomodata: e intanto portale questa
uncomfortable and in the meantime carry her this
(ill)

stiacciata e questo vasetto di burro".
focaccio and this little vase of butter
(unleavened bread) (jar)

Cappuccetto Rosso, senza farselo dire due
Little hood Red without to make herself it tell two

volte, partì per andare dalla sua nonna, la
times left for to go from the her grandmother -the-
(to)

quale stava in un altro villaggio. E passando per
which was in an other village And passing by
(who)

un bosco s'imbatté in quella buona lana del
a forest himself ran into in that good wool of the
{ironic} (sheep) (of a)

Lupo, il quale avrebbe avuto una gran voglia di
Wolf the which would have had a great desire of

mangiarsela; ma poi non ebbe il coraggio di
to eat himself her but then not (he) had the courage of

farlo, a motivo di certi taglialegna che erano
to do it at motive of (a) certain woodcutter that was

lì nella foresta.
there in the forest

Egli le domandò dove andava.
He her asked where (she) went

La povera bambina, che non sapeva quanto sia
The poor girl that not knew how much is

pericoloso fermarsi per dar retta al Lupo, gli
dangerous to stop herself to give right to the Wolf him
pay attention

disse:
said

"Vo a vedere la mia nonna e a portarle
(I) go to see -the- my grandmother and to bring her
{literary}

una stiacciata, con questo vasetto di burro, che le
a focaccia with this jar of butter that her

manda la mamma mia".
sends -the- mamma (of) mine

"Sta molto lontana di qui?", disse il Lupo.
(It) is very far of here said the Wolf

"Oh, altro!", disse Cappuccetto Rosso. "La sta
Oh else said Little hood Red It is

laggiù, passato quel mulino, che si vede di
down there past that mill that itself sees from

qui, nella prima casa, al principio del villaggio."
here in the first house at the beginning of the village

"Benissimo", disse il Lupo, "voglio venire a vederla
Very well said the Wolf (I) want to come to see her

anch'io. Io piglierò da questa parte, e tu da
also I — I — will take — by — this — part — and — you — of
(will go)

quell'altra, e faremo a chi arriva più presto."
that other — and — (we) do — at — who — arrives — most — soon

Il Lupo si messe a correre per la sua
The — Wolf — himself — put — to — run — by — -the- — his

strada, che era una scorciatoia, con quanta forza
street — that — was — a — shortcut — with — as much — power

avea nelle gambe: e la bambina se ne andò
(he) had — in the — legs — and — the — child — itself — of it — went

per la sua strada, che era la più lunga,
by — the — his — street — that — was — the — most — long

baloccandosi a cogliere le nocciuole, a dar
amusing herself — to — catch — -the- — nuts — to — give
(nocciole) (go)

dietro alle farfalle, e a fare dei mazzetti con
after — -to the- — butterflies — and — to — make — of the — bunches — with

tutti i fiorellini, che incontrava lungo la via.
all — the — little flowers — that — (he) encountered — along — the — way

Il Lupo in due salti arrivò a casa della
The Wolf in two jumps arrived at (the) house of the

nonna e bussò.
grandma and knocked

"Toc, toc."
Knock knock

"Chi è?"
Who is (it)

"Sono la vostra bambina, son Cappuccetto
(I) am -the- your child (I) am Little hood

Rosso", disse il Lupo, contraffacendone la voce,
Red said the Wolf counter-doing the voice
(changing)

"e vengo a portarvi una stiacciata e un
and (I) come to carry you a focaccio and a
(unleavened bread)

vasetto di burro, che vi manda la mamma mia."
jar of butter that you sends the mother (of) mine

La buona nonna, che era a letto perché non
The good grandmother that was at bed because not
(who) (in the)

si   sentiva troppo bene, gli gridò:
himself (he) felt very   well him shouted

"Tira la stanghetta, e la porta si aprirà".
Pull the little bar and the door itself will open

Il Lupo tirò la stanghetta, e la porta si
The Wolf pulled the little bar and the door itself

aprì. Appena dentro, si gettò sulla buona
opened Hardly inside himself (he) threw on the good

donna e la divorò in men che non si dice,
woman and her devoured in less than not oneself says

perché erano tre giorni che non s'era
because (there) were three days that not itself was

sdigiunato. Quindi rinchiuse la porta e andò a
breakfasted Then close the door and went to

mettersi nel letto della nonna, aspettando che
set himself in the bed of the grandmother waiting for that
(until)

arrivasse Cappuccetto Rosso, che, di lì a poco,
arrived Little hood Red that from there to little

venne a picchiare alla porta.
came to knock at the door

"Toc, toc."
Knock knock

"Chi è?"
Who is (it)

Cappuccetto Rosso, che sentì il vocione grosso
Little hood Red that heard the voice great

del Lupo, ebbe dapprincipio un po' di paura; ma
of the Wolf had at the beginning a bit of fear but

credendo che la sua nonna fosse infreddata
believing that -the- her grandma was having a cold

rispose:
answered

"Sono la vostra bambina, son Cappuccetto
(I) am -the- your child (I) am Little hood

Rosso, che vengo a portarvi una stiacciata e un
Red that (I) come to bring you a focaccio and a

vasetto di burro, che vi manda la mamma mia".
jar   of butter that you sends the mother (of) mine

Il   Lupo gridò di dentro, assottigliando un po' la
The Wolf shouted of inside   thinning   a bit the

voce:
voice

"Tira la stanghetta e la porta si aprirà."
Pull the little bar and her carried itself will open

Cappuccetto Rosso tirò la stanghetta e la
Little hood   Red   pulled the little bar   and the

porta si aprì.
door itself opened

Il   Lupo, vistala entrare, le disse, nascondendosi
The Wolf seen her enter   her said   hiding himself
          (seeing her)

sotto le coperte:
under the covers

"Posa la stiacciata e il vasetto di burro sulla
Put   the focaccia (bread) and the   jar   of butter on the

madia   e   vieni a letto con me".
kneading trough and come to bed with me

Cappuccetto Rosso si   spogliò ed entrò nel
Little hood   Red   herself undressed and entered in the

letto, dove ebbe una gran sorpresa nel vedere
bed where (he) had a great surprise in the to see

com'era fatta la sua nonna, quando era
how was made -the- her grandmother when (she) was

tutta spogliata. E cominciò a dire:
all undressed And (she) began to say

"O nonna mia, che braccia grandi che
Oh grandmother (of) mine what arms large -that-
                              {plural}

avete!".
(you) have

"Gli è per abbracciarti meglio, bambina mia."
It is for to embrace you better child (of) mine
                              {feminine}

"O nonna mia, che gambe grandi che
Oh grandmother (of) mine what legs large -that-
                              {plural}

avete!"
(you) have

"Gli è per correr meglio, bambina mia."
It is for   to run   better   child   (of) mine
                                          {feminine}

"O   nonna   mia,   che   orecchie grandi che
Oh grandmother (of) mine what   ears   large   that
                                          {plural}

avete!"
(you) have

"Gli è per sentirci meglio, bambina mia."
It is for to hear you better   child   (of) mine
                                      {feminine}

"O   nonna   mia,   che occhioni grandi   che
Oh grandmother (of) mine what   eyes   large   -that-
                                      {plural}

avete!"
(you) have

"Gli è per vederci meglio, bambina mia."
It is for to see you better   child   (of) mine
                                    {feminine}

"O   nonna   mia,   che denti grandi   che
Oh grandmother (of) mine what teeth   large   -that-
                                    {plural}

avete!"
(you) have

"Gli è per mangiarti meglio."
It is for to eat you better

E nel dir così, quel malanno di Lupo si
And in -the- to say like so that scoundrel of (a) Wolf himself

gettò sul povero Cappuccetto Rosso, e ne
threw on the poor Little hood Red and of her

fece un boccone.
made a mouthful

La storia di Cappuccetto Rosso fa vedere ai
The story of Little hood Red makes see to the

giovinetti e alle giovinette, e segnatamente
male youths and to the female youths and especially
(boys) (girls)

alle giovinette, che non bisogna mai
at the female youths that not (it is) necessary ever
(girls)

fermarsi a discorrere per la strada con
to stop themselves to talk on the street with

gente che non si conosce: perché dei lupi
people that not oneself (one) knows because -of the- wolves

ce n'è dappertutto e di diverse specie, e i
there of it is everywhere and of diverse sorts and the

più pericolosi sono appunto quelli che hanno
most dangerous are especially those that have

faccia di persone garbate e piene di
face of persons polite and full of
(the aspect) (a person)

complimenti e di belle maniere.
compliments and of nice manners

Le Fate

Le Fate
The Fairies

C'era **una** **volta** **una** **vedova** **che** **aveva** **due**
There was one time a widow that had two

figliuole. **La** **maggiore** **somigliava** **tutta** **alla**
daughters The elder seemed all to the

mamma, **di** **lineamenti** **e** **di** **carattere,** **e** **chi**
mamma of features and of character and who

vedeva **lei,** **vedeva** **sua** **madre,** **tale** **e** **quale. Tutte**
saw her saw her mother such and which All

e **due** **erano** **tanto** **antipatiche** **e** **così** **gonfie** **di**
and two were so much unpleasant and so swollen of

superbia, **che** **nessuno** **le** **voleva** **avvicinare.**
pride that no one her wanted to approach

15

Viverci insieme poi, era impossibile addirittura.
To live there together then was impossible directly

La più giovane invece, per la dolcezza dei
The most young instead for the sweetness of the

modi e per la bontà del cuore, era tutta il
manners and for the goodness of the heart was all the

ritratto del suo babbo... e tanto bella poi,
portrait of -the- her father and so much beautiful then

tanto bella, che non si sarebbe trovata
so beautiful that not oneself would be found

l'eguale. E naturalmente, poiché ogni simile ama
the equal And naturally since each similar soul

il suo simile, quella madre andava pazza per la
-the- her similar that mother went crazy by the
(equal)

figliuola maggiore; e sentiva per quell'altra
daughter elder and felt for that other

un'avversione, una ripugnanza spaventevole. La
an aversion a repugnance fearful Her

faceva mangiare in cucina, e tutte le fatiche
made to eat in (the) kitchen and all the fatigues

e i servizi di casa toccavano a lei.
and the services of (the) house touched to her
(were given)

Fra le altre cose, bisognava che quella povera
Between the other things needed that that poor

ragazza andasse due volte al giorno ad attingere
girl went two times at the day to attain
(get)

acqua a una fontana distante più d'un miglio e
water at a fountain distant more of a mile and

mezzo, e ne riportasse una brocca piena.
(a) half and of it brought back a pitcher full

Un giorno, mentre stava appunto lì alla
One day while (he) stood exactly there at the

fonte, le apparve accanto una povera vecchia che
fountain her appeared beside a poor old lady that

la pregò in carità di darle da bere.
her (she) asked in charity of to give her of to drink

"Ma volentieri, nonnina mia..." rispose la bella
But   voluntarily   granny   (of) mine   answered   the   beautiful

fanciulla "aspettate; vi sciacquo la brocca..."
girl   wait   you   flush   the   pitcher
                     (fill)

E subito dette alla mezzina una bella
And   immediately   gave   to the   half   a   beautiful

risciacquata, la riempì di acqua fresca, e gliela
rinse   it   refilled   of   water   fresh   and   her it

presentò sostenendola in alto con le sue proprie
presented   supporting it   in   high   with   -the-   her   own

mani, affinché la vecchiarella bevesse con tutto
hands   until   the   old woman   drank   with   all

il suo comodo.
-the-   her   comfort

Quand'ebbe bevuto, disse la nonnina:
When (she) had   drunk   said   the   granny

"Tu sei tanto bella, quanto buona e quanto per
You   are   so   beautiful   as much   good   and   as much   for

benino, figliuola mia, che non posso fare a
pretty daughter (of) mine that not (I) can do at

meno di lasciarti un dono".
least of to leave you a gift

Quella era una Fata, che aveva preso la forma di
That was a Fairy that had taken the form of

una povera vecchia di campagna per vedere
a poor old woman of (the) countryside for to see

fin dove arrivava la bontà della giovinetta. E
until where arrived the goodness of the young woman And

continuò:
(he) continued

"Ti do per dono che ad ogni parola che
You (I) give as gift that at each word that

pronunzierai ti esca di bocca o un fiore o
(you) shalt speak you exit of mouth or a flower or
(either)

una pietra preziosa".
a stone precious

La ragazza arrivò a casa con la brocca piena,
The girl arrived at (the) house with the pitcher full

qualche minuto più tardi; la mamma le fece un
some minute more late the mother her made a

baccano del diavolo per quel piccolo ritardo.
din of the devil for that small delay

"Mamma, abbi pazienza, ti domando scusa...", disse
Mamma have patience you (I) ask excuse said

la figliuola tutta umile, e intanto che parlava
the girl all humble and while that (she) talked

le uscirono di bocca due rose, due perle e
her came out of (the) mouth two roses two perls and

due brillanti grossi.
two diamonds large

"Ma che roba è questa!...", esclamò la madre
But what thing is this exclaimed the mother

stupefatta, "sbaglio o tu sputi perle e
stupefied (I) mistake or you spit perls and
(am I mistaken)

brillanti!... O come mai, figlia mia?..."
diamonds Oh how ever daughter (of) mine

Era la prima volta in tutta la sua vita che la
(It) was the first time in all -the- her life that her

chiamava così, e in tono affettuoso. La fanciulla
(she) called like that and in tone affectionate The girl

raccontò ingenuamente quel che le era accaduto
told naively that what her was happened
(had)

alla fontana; e durante il racconto, figuratevi
at the fountain and during the story figure yourself

i rubini e i topazi che le caddero già
the rubies and the topazes that her fell already

dalla bocca!
from the mouth

"Oh, che fortuna...", disse la madre, "bisogna
Oh what fortune said the mather (it is) necessary

che ci mandi subito anche quest'altra. Senti,
that there (I) send immediately also this other Hear

Cecchina, guarda che cosa esce dalla bocca
Cecchina   guard   what   thing comes out of the   mouth

della tua sorella quando parla. Ti piacerebbe
of -the- your sister   when   (she) talks You (it) would please

avere anche per te lo stesso dono?... Basta che
to have   also   for you the   same   gift   Enough that

tu vada alla fonte; e se una vecchia ti
you   go to the fountain and if   an old woman you

chiede da bere, daglielo con buona maniera."
asks   of to drink give her it with   good   manner(s)

"E non ci mancherebbe altro!...", rispose quella
And not us   would lack (anything) else answered   that
                As if we need to

sbadata. "Andare alla fontana ora!"
careless (girl) To go   to the fountain now

"Ti dico che tu ci vada... e subito", gridò
You (I) say that you there   go   and immediately shouted

la mamma.
the   mother

Brontolò, brontolò; ma brontolando prese la
(she) grumbled grumbled but grumbling took the

strada portando con sé la più bella fiasca
street taking with herself the most beautiful flask

d'argento che fosse in casa. La superbia,
of silver that was in (the) house The pride

capite, e l'infingardaggine!... Appena arrivata
understand and the sloth Hardly arrived

alla fonte, eccoti apparire una gran signora
at the fountain see here appear a great lady

vestita magnificamente, che le chiede un sorso
dressed magnificently that her asked a sip

d'acqua. Era la medesima Fata apparsa poco
of water (It) was the same Fairy (who) appeared (a) little

prima a quell'altra sorella; ma aveva preso
before to that other sister but (she) had taken

l'aspetto e il vestiario di una principessa, per
the appearance and the dress of a princess for

vedere fino a quale punto giungeva la malcreanza
to see until to which point arrived the rudeness

di quella pettegola.
of that gossip

"O sta' a vedere...", rispose la superba, "che son
Oh stand to see answered the prideful one that are

venuta qui per dar da bere a voi!... Sicuro!...
come here for to give of to drink to you Sure

per abbeverare vostra Signora, non per altro!...
for to quench your Ladyship not for (anything) else

Guardate, se avete sete, la fonte eccola lì."
Watch if (you) have thirst the fountain see her there

"Avete poca educazione, ragazza...", rispose la
(You) have little education girl answered the

Fata senza adirarsi punto, "e giacché
Fairy without to get herself angry exactly and as

siete così sgarbata, vi do per dono che ad
(you) are so unkind you (I) give as gift that at

ogni parola pronunziata da voi vi esca di
each word pronounced from you you comes out of

bocca un rospo o una serpe."
(the) mouth a toad or a snake

Appena la mammina la vide tornare da lontano,
Hardly the little mother her saw return from afar

le gridò a piena gola:
her yelled at full throat

"Dunque, Cecchina, com'è andata?".
Therefore Cecchina how is (it) gone
(So!)

"Non mi seccate, mamma!...", replicò la monella; e
Not me bother mother replied the gamine and
Don't bother me

sputò due vipere e due rospacci.
spit two vipers and two ugly toads

"O Dio!... che vedo!...", esclamò la madre. "La colpa
Oh God what (do I) see exclaimed the mother The fault

deve essere tutta di tua sorella, ma me la
must be all of your sister but me it

pagherà..."
(she) will pay

E   si   mosse   per   picchiarla. Quella povera
And   herself (she) moved for   to beat her   That   poor

figliuola fuggì   via   di   rincorsa   e   andò   a
daughter   fled   away   of   (the) chase and   went   to

rifugiarsi   nella foresta vicina.
shelter herself in the   forest   close by

Il   figliuolo del   Re   che ritornava   da   caccia   la
The   son   of the King that   returned   from (the) hunt her

incontrò   per   un   viottolo,   e   vedendola   così
encountered   by   a   little path   and   seeing her   so

bella,   le   domandò   che cosa faceva in quel luogo
beautiful her   asked   what thing (she) did in   that   place

sola sola,   e   perché piangeva tanto.
alone alone and because (she) cried so much
  all alone

"La   mamma...", disse lei, "m'ha mandato via   di
The   mother   said   she   me has   send   away   from

casa   e mi voleva picchiare..."
(the) house and me wants   to beat

Il   figliuolo del   Re, che vide uscire   da   quella
The   son   of the King that saw come out from   that

bocchina   cinque o sei perle e altrettanti brillanti,
little mouth   five   or six perls and   various   diamonds

la   pregò di raccontare come mai   era   possibile
her   asked   of   to tell   how   ever (it) was possible

una   cosa   tanto   meravigliosa.   E   la   ragazza
a   thing   so   wondrous   And   the   girl

raccontò per filo   e per segno tutto quello che
  told   by thread and by   sign   all   that   what

le era accaduto.
her was   happened
     (had)

Il   Principe reale   se   ne   innamorò   subito
The   Prince   royal himself with her fell in love immediately

e   considerando che il dono della Fata   valeva
and   considering   that the gift of the Fairy was worth

più   di   qualunque grossa dote che potesse avere
more of   any   big   dowry that could   have
(than)

un'altra donna, la condusse   senz'altro   al
another woman her   led   without other to the
(without hesitation)

palazzo del Re suo padre e   se   la sposò.
palace of the King his father and himself her married

Quell'altra sorella frattanto si   fece talmente
That other   sister meanwhile herself made   so

odiare da tutti, che sua madre stessa la cacciò
hate   of   all   that her mother (her)self her chased

via di casa; e la disgraziata dopo aver
away from (the) house and the disgraced one after to have

corso invano cercando chi acconsentisse a
run   in vain searching who   consented   to
(that would consent)

riceverla andò a morire sul confine del bosco.
receive her went to die at the edge of the forest

MORALE
Moral

Gli smeraldi, le perle, ed i diamanti
The emeralds the perls and the diamonds

Abbaglian gli occhi col vivo splendore;
dazzl' the eyes with -the- lively splendor

Ma le dolci parole e i dolci pianti
But the sweet words and the sweet cries

Hanno spesso più forza e più valore.
Have often more force and more value

ALTRA MORALE
Other Moral

La cortesia che le bell'alme accende,
The curtesy that the good soul lights

Costa talora acerbi affanni e pene;
Costs sometimes unripe cares and pains

Ma presto o tardi la virtù risplende,
But soon or late the virtue shines
(sooner) (later)

E quando men ci pensa il premio ottiene.
And when less one thinks the prize obtains

Barba-blu

Barba-blu
Beard-blue
(Blue Beard)

C'era una volta un uomo, il quale aveva palazzi
There was one time a man the which had palaces

e ville principesche, e piatte d'oro e
and towns princely and plates of gold and

d'argento, e mobilia di lusso ricamata, e
of silver and furniture of luxury embroidered and

carrozze tutte dorate di dentro e di fuori.
carriages all golden of inside and of outside

Ma quest'uomo, per sua disgrazia, aveva la barba
But this man for his disgrace had the beard

blu: e questa cosa lo faceva così brutto e
blue and this thing him made so ugly and

spaventoso, che non c'era donna, ragazza o
fearful   that   not there was (a) woman girl or

maritata, che soltanto a vederlo, non fuggisse
married lady that only to see him not escaped

a gambe dalla paura.
at legs from the fear
  very fast

Fra le sue vicinanti, c'era una gran dama,
Between -the- his neighbors there was a great lady

la quale aveva due figlie, due occhi di sole. Egli
the which had two girls two eyes of sun He

ne chiese una in moglie, lasciando alla madre la
of it asked one in wife leaving to the mother the
    (as)

scelta di quella delle due che avesse voluto
choice of the one of the two that (she) had wanted

dargli: ma le ragazze non volevano saperne
to give him but the girls not wanted to know of it

nulla: e se lo palleggiavano dall'una all'altra,
nothing and if it bandied from the one to the other

non trovando il verso di risolversi a
not finding the direction of to resolve themselves to

sposare un uomo, che aveva la barba blu. La
marry a man that had the beard blue The

cosa poi che più di tutto faceva loro ribrezzo era
thing after that most of all made their disgust was

quella, che quest'uomo aveva sposato diverse
that that this man had married various

donne e di queste non s'era mai potuto
women and of these not itself was ever been able
(possible)

sapere che cosa fosse accaduto.
to know what thing was happened
(had)

Fatto sta che Barba-blu, tanto per entrare in
Fact is that Beard-blue, so much for to enter in
(Blue Beard)

relazione, le menò, insieme alla madre e a
relation her led together to the mother and at
(with the) (with)

tre o quattro delle loro amiche e in
three or four of -the- their friends and in

compagnia di alcuni giovinotti del vicinato, in
company of any youths of the neighborhood in

una sua villa, dove si trattennero otto
one (of) his villa(s) where themselves were held eight

giorni interi. E lì, fu tutto un metter su
days entire And there was all a to put on

passeggiate, partite di caccia e di pesca, balli,
walks games of (a) hunt and of fish dances

festini, merende: nessuno trovò il tempo per
feasts snacks no one found the time for

chiudere un occhio, perché passavano le nottate
to close an eye because (they) passed the nights

a farsi fra loro delle celie: insomma,
to make themselves between them of the jokes in sum

le cose presero una così buona piega, che la
the things took a so good fold that the
(twist)

figlia minore finì col persuadersi che il
daughter younger finished with the to persuade herself that the

padrone della villa non aveva la barba tanto blu,
master of the villa not had the beard so blue

e che era una persona ammodo e molto
and that (he) was a person nice and very

perbene. Tornati di campagna,
proper Returned from (the) countryside

si fecero le nozze.
themselves made the nuptials
they married

In capo a un mese, Barba-blu disse a sua moglie
In head at a month Beard-blue said to his wife
At the end of (Blue Beard)

che per un affare di molta importanza era
that for an affair of much importance (he) was

costretto a mettersi in viaggio e a restar fuori
forced to put himself in travel and to stay outside

almeno sei settimane: che la pregava di stare
at least six weeks that her (he) asked of to be

allegra, durante la sua assenza; che invitasse
happy during -the- his absence that (she) invited
(she could invite)

le	sue	amiche	del	cuore,	che	le	menasse	in
-the-	her	friends	of the	heart	that	them	(she) take	in

campagna,	caso	le	avesse	fatto	piacere:	in	una
(the) countryside	(in) case	her	(it) had	made	pleasure	in	one

parola,	che	trattasse	da	regina	e	tenesse
word	that	(she) treated	of	queen	and	keep
		(she acted)	(as)			

dappertutto	corte	bandita.
everywhere	court	proclamation
	a well set table	

"Ecco",	le	disse,	"le	chiavi	delle	due	grandi
See	her	(he) said	the	keys	of the	two	great
(Here)							

guardarobe:	ecco	quella	dei	piatti	d'oro	e
wardrobes	see	that	of the	plates	of gold	and

d'argento,	che	non	vanno	in	opera	tutti	i	giorni:
of silver	that	not	go	in	work	all	the	days

ecco	quella	dei	miei	scrigni,	dove	tengo	i
see	that	of the	my	coffers	where	(I) keep	the

sacchi	delle	monete:	ecco	quella	degli	astucci,
sacks	of -the-	money	see	that	of the	small cases
			(here)			

dove sono le gioie e i finimenti di pietre
where are the jewels and the finishings of stones
(encasings)

preziose: ecco la chiave comune, che serve per
precious see the key generic that serves for

aprire tutti i quartieri. Quanto poi a quest'altra
to open all the rooms When after the this other

chiavicina qui, è quella della stanzina, che rimane
little key here is that of the little room that remains

in fondo al gran corridoio del pian terreno.
in (the) back to the large corridor of the flat terrain
ground floor

Padrona di aprir tutto, di andar dappertutto: ma
Master of to open all of to go everywhere but

in quanto alla piccola stanzina, vi proibisco
in as much to the small little room you (I) prohibit

d'entrarvi e ve lo proibisco in modo così
of to enter yourself and you it (I) prohibit in manner so

assoluto, che se vi accadesse per disgrazia di
absolute that if you happen by disgrace of

aprirla, potete aspettarvi tutto dalla mia
to open it (you) can expect yourself all of -the- my

collera."
anger

Ella promette che sarebbe stata attaccata agli
She promised that (she) would been attached to the
(obeying)

ordini: ed egli, dopo averla abbracciata, monta
orders and he after to have her hugged mounted
(climbed)

in carrozza, e via per il suo viaggio.
in(to) (the) carriage and went for -the- his journey

Le vicine e le amiche non aspettarono di
The neighbors and the friends not expected -of-

essere cercate, per andare dalla sposa novella,
to be searched for to go of the spouse new
(to the)

tanto si struggevano dalla voglia di vedere
so much themselves pined of the wish of to see

tutte le magnificenze del suo palazzo, non
all the wonders of -the- his palace not

essendosi   arrisicate di andarci prima, quando
being themselves   risked   of   to go there   first   when

c'era   sempre   il   marito,   a   motivo   di   quella
there was   always   the   husband   at   motive   of   that

barba   blu,   che   faceva   loro   tanta   paura.   Ed
beard   blue   that   made   them   so much   fear   And
                    (gave)

eccole   subito   a   vagare   per   le   sale,   per
see them   immediately   to   roam   through   the   halls   through

le   camere   e   per   le   gallerie,   sempre   di
the   rooms   and   through   the   galleries   always   from

meraviglia   in   meraviglia.   Salite   di   sopra,   nelle
wonder   in(to)   wonder   Climbed   of   up   in the

stanze   di   guardaroba,   andarono   in   visibilio   nel
rooms   of   wardrobe   (they) went   in   visibility   in the

vedere   la   bellezza   e   la   gran   quantità   dei
to see   the   beauty   and   the   great   quantity   of the

parati,   dei   tappeti,   dei   letti,   delle   tavole,   dei
walls   of the   rugs   of the   beds   of the   tables   of the

tavolini da lavoro, e dei grandi specchi, dove
little tables of work and of the great mirrors where

uno si poteva mirare dalla punta dei piedi
one oneself could watch from the point of the feet

fino ai capelli, e le cui cornici, parte di
until to the hairs and the which horns part of

cristallo e parte d'argento e d'argento dorato,
crystal and part of silver and of silver golden

erano la cosa più bella e più sorprendente
were the thing most beautiful and most surprising

che si fosse mai veduta. Esse non rifinivano dal
that itself was ever seen These not finished of the

magnificare e dall'invidiare la felicità della loro
to magnify and of the envy the happiness of the their
(glorifying) (being jealous of)

amica, la quale, invece, non si divertiva punto
friend the which instead not himself amused exactly

alla vista di tante ricchezze, tormentata,
at the view of so many riches tormented

com'era,   dalla   gran   curiosità   di   andare   a   vedere
like (she) was   by the   great   curiosity   of   to go   to   see

la   stanzina   del   pian   terreno.
the   little room   of the   ground   floor

E   non   potendo   più   stare   alle   mosse,   senza
And   not   being able   more   to be   at the   moves   without

badare   alla   sconvenienza   di   lasciar   lì   su   due
to watch   at the   inconvenience   of   to let   there   on   two

piedi   tutta   la   compagnia,   prese   per   una   scaletta
pieces   all   the   company   took   -by-   a   little stair

segreta,   e   scese   giù   con   tanta   furia,   che
secret   and   descended   down   with   so much   fury   that

due   o   tre   volte   ci   corse   poco   non
two   or   three   times   there   ran   little   not
*   almost*

si   rompesse   l'osso   del   collo.
herself   broke   the bone   of the   neck
*   breaking   the neck*

Arrivata   all'uscio   della   stanzina,   si   fermò   un
Arrived   at the exit   of the   little room   himself   stopped   a

momento, ripensando alla proibizione del marito,
moment   rethinking   to the   prohibition   of the   husband
(of the)

e per la paura dei guai, ai quali poteva
and for the fear of the trouble at the which (she) could

andare incontro per la sua disubbidienza: ma la
go   towards   for -the- her   disobedience   but the

tentazione fu così potente, che non ci fu
tentation   was so   powerful   that not there was

modo di vincerla. Prese dunque la chiave, e
manner of to conquer it (She) took therefore the   key   and

tremando come una foglia aprì l'uscio della
trembling   like a   leaf   (she) opened the door of the

stanzina.
little room

Dapprincipio non poté distinguere nulla
From the beginning   not (she) could   distinguish   nothing

perché le finestre erano chiuse: ma a poco a
because the windows were closed but -at- little at
(by)

poco	cominciò	a	vedere	che	il	pavimento	era
little	(she) began	to	see	that	the	floor	was

tutto	coperto	di	sangue	accagliato,	dove	si
all	covered	of	blood	coagulated	where	themselves

riflettevano	i	corpi	di	parecchie	donne	morte	e
reflected	the	corpses	of	several	women	dead	and

attaccate	in	giro	alle	pareti.	Erano	tutte	le
attached	in	round / all around	to the	walls	(They) were	all	the

donne	che	Barba-blu	aveva	sposate,	eppoi
women	that	Barba-blue (Blue Beard)	had	married	and then

sgozzate,	una	dietro	l'altra.
slaughtered	one	after	the other

Se	non	morì	dalla	paura,	fu	un	miracolo:
If	not	(she) died	from the	fear	(it) was	a	miracle

e	la	chiave	della	stanzina,	che	essa	aveva
and	the	key	of the	little room	that	she	had

ritirato	fuori	dal	buco	della	porta,	le	cascò
pulled back	out	from the	hole	of the	door	her	fell

di   mano.
from (the) hand

Quando   si   fu   riavuta un poco,   raccattò
When   herself (she) was found back a   bit   (she) retrieved
                 (she had)

la chiave, richiuse   la porticina   e   salì   nella
the key   closed again the little door and exited in -the-

sua camera, per   rimettersi   dallo   spavento: ma
her room   for   to mend herself   from the fear   but

era   tanto   commossa   e   agitata,   che   non
(she) was so much   affected   and agitated   that not

trovava   la via a pigliar   fiato   e   a rifare un
(she) found the way to catch   (her) breath and to redo   a
                                                       · (get)

po' di colore.
bit of   color

Essendosi avvista che   la chiave della   stanzina   si
Being herself seen   that the key   of the   little room itself
     Seeing

era macchiata di sangue, la   ripulì   due o tre
was stained   of   blood   it cleaned again two or three

volte:	ma	il	sangue	non	voleva	andar	via.	Ebbe
times	but	the	blood	not	wanted	to go	away	(She) had

un	bel	lavarla	e	un	bello	strofinarla	colla	rena
a	nice	to clean it	and	a	nice	to rub it	with the	sand

e	col	gesso:	il	sangue	era	sempre	lì:
and	with the	plaster	the	blood	was	always	there

perché	la	chiave	era	fatata	e	non	c'era
because	the	key	was	enchanted	and	not	there was

verso	di	pulirla	perbene:	quando	il	sangue
(a) verse (a way)	of	to clean it	proper	when	the	blood

spariva	da	una	parte,	rifioriva	subito	da
disappeared	of (on)	one	part	(it) rebloomed	immediately	of (on)

quell'altra.
that other
(some other part)

Barba-blu	tornò	dal	suo	viaggio	quella
Beard-blue (Blue Beard)	returned	from -the-	his	journey	that

sera	stessa,	raccontando	che	per	la	strada
evening same	same	recounting	that	by (on)	the	street
	evening					

aveva
(he) had

ricevuto lettere, dove gli dicevano che l'affare, per
received letters where him (they) told that the affair for

il quale si era dovuto muovere da
-the- which himself (he) was had to move from
(he had)

casa, era stato bell'e accomodato e in modo
(the) house was been well and accomodated and in manner
(had)

vantaggioso per lui.
advantageous for him

La moglie fece tutto quello che poté per
The wife did all that what (she) could for

dargli ad intendere che era oltremodo
to give him to understand that (she) was otherwise

contenta del suo sollecito ritorno.
happy of -the- his prompt return

Il giorno dipoi il marito le richiese le
The day afterwards the husband (from) her requested the

chiavi: ed ella gliele consegnò: ma la sua
keys and she him them consigned but -the- her
(gave)

mano tremava tanto, che esso poté indovinare
hand trembled so much that he could guess

senza fatica tutto l'accaduto.
without fatigue all that happened

"Come va", diss'egli, "che fra tutte queste chiavi
How goes said he that between all these keys

non ci trovo quella della stanzina?"
not it found that of the little room

"Si vede", ella rispose, "che l'avrò lasciata
One sees she answered that it (I) will have left

disopra, sul mio tavolino."
upstairs on the my little table

"Badate bene", disse Barba-blu, "che la voglio
Take heed well said Beard-blue that it (I) want
(Blue Beard)

subito."
immediately

Riuscito inutile ogni pretesto per
Succeeded useless each pretext for
(Turned out to be)

traccheggiare,   convenne   portar   la   chiave.
temporize   agreed   to carry   the   key
(to delay)

Barba-blu,   dopo   averci   messo   sopra   gli   occhi,
Beard-blue   after   to have it   put   on   the   eyes
(Blue Beard)

domandò   alla   moglie:
asked   to the   wife

"Come mai su questa chiave   c'è   del   sangue?".
How   ever   on   this   key   there is   of the   blood

"Non lo   so   davvero", rispose   la   povera donna,
Not   it   (I) know   really   answered   the   poor   woman

più   bianca   della   morte.
more   white   of the   death
                (than the)

"Ah! non lo   sapete,   eh!", replicò Barba-blu, "ma lo
Ah   not   it   (you) know   eh   replied   Beard-blue   but   it
                                  (Blue Beard)

so   ben io! Voi siete voluta entrare nella stanzina.
know   well   I   You   are   wanted   to enter   in the   little room

Ebbene,   o   signora: voi   ci   entrerete per sempre
And well   oh   lady   you   there   (you) enter   for   always
(Well)

e andrete a pigliar posto accanto a quelle
and (you) will go to take (a) place next to those

altre donne, che avete veduto là dentro."
other women that had seen there inside

Ella si gettò ai piedi di suo marito
She herself threw at the feet of her husband

piangendo e chiedendo perdono, con tutti i
crying and asking pardon with all the

segni di un vero pentimento, dell'aver
signs of a true repentance of the to have

disubbidito. Bella e addolorata com'era,
disobeyed Beautiful and pained like (she) was

avrebbe intenerito un macigno: ma Barba-blu
(she) would have softened a boulder but Beard-blue
(Blue Beard)

aveva il cuore più duro del macigno.
had the heart more hard of the boulder
(than a)

"Bisogna morire, signora", diss'egli, "e subito."
(You) need to die lady said he and immediately

"Poiché mi tocca a morire", ella rispose
Since me (it) touches to die she answered

guardandolo con due occhi tutti pieni di pianto,
watching it with two eyes all full of cry
(tears)

"datemi almeno il tempo di raccomandarmi a
give me at least the time of to recommend myself to

Dio."
God

"Vi accordo un mezzo quarto d'ora: non un
You (I) grant a half quarter of hour not a

minuto di più", replicò il marito.
minute of more answered the husband

Appena rimasta sola, chiamò la sua sorella e
Hardly remained alone (she) called -the- her sister and

le disse:
her said

"Anna", era questo il suo nome, "Anna, sorella
Anna was this -the- her name Anna sister

mia, ti prego, sali su in cima alla torre per
(of) mine | you | (I) ask | go out | up | in | top | to the | tower | for

vedere se per caso arrivassero i miei fratelli; mi
to see | if | by | case | arrived | -the- | my | brothers | me

hanno promesso che oggi sarebbero venuti a
have | promised | that | today | (they) would | come | to

trovarmi; se li vedi, fa' loro segno, perché
find me | if | there | (you) see | make | them | (a) sign | because
(so that)

si affrettino a più non posso".
they | haste | to | more | not | (I) can

La sorella Anna salì in cima alla torre e la
The | sister | Anna | went up | in | top | to the | tower | and | the
(on) | (of the)

povera sconsolata le gridava
poor | disconsolate (girl) | her | yelled at

di tanto in tanto:
of | so much | in | so much
now and then

"Anna, Anna, sorella mia, non vedi tu apparir
Anna | Anna | sister | (of) mine | not | see | you | appear

nessuno?".
no one

"Non vedo altro che il sole che fiammeggia e
Not (I) see other than the sun that flames and

l'erba che verdeggia."
the grass that grows green

Intanto Barba-blu, con un gran coltellaccio in
Meanwhile Beard-blue with a great knife in
(Blue Beard)

mano, gridava con quanta ne aveva ne'
hand shouted with as much as of it (he) had in the

polmoni:
lungs

"Scendi subito! o se no, salgo io".
Get down immediately or if not come up I

"Un altro minuto, per carità" rispondeva la moglie.
An other minute for charity responded the wife
have mercy

E di nuovo si metteva a gridare con voce
And of new herself (she) set to shout with voice

soffocata:
suffocated

"Anna, Anna, sorella mia, non vedi tu apparir
Anna   Anna   sister   (of) mine   not   see   you   appear

nessuno?".
no one

"Non vedo altro che il sole che fiammeggia e
Not   (I) see   other   than   the   sun   that   flames   and

l'erba che verdeggia."
the grass   that   grows green

"Spicciati a scendere", urlava Barba-blu, "o se no
Hurry up   to   go down   screamed   Beard-blue   or   if   not
                (Blue Beard)

salgo io."
go up   I

"Eccomi" rispondeva sua moglie; e daccapo a
See me   answered   his   wife   and   of-head   to
               (started)

gridare:
yell

"Anna, Anna, sorella mia, non vedi tu apparir
Anna   Anna   sister   (of) mine   not   see   you   appear

nessuno?".
no one

"Vedo" rispose la sorella Anna "vedo un gran
(I) see   answered   the   sister   Anna   (I) see   a   great

polverone che viene verso questa parte..."
(cloud of) dust   that   comes   towards   this   side

"Sono forse i miei fratelli? "
Are (they)   maybe   -the-   my   brothers

"Ohimè no, sorella mia: è un branco di
Oh my   no   sister   (of) mine   (it) is   a   herd   of

montoni."
rams
(sheep)

"Insomma vuoi scendere, sì o no?", urlava
In sum   do (you) want   to go down   yes   or   no   shouted

Barba-blu.
Beard-blue
(Blue Beard)

"Un'altro momentino" rispondeva la moglie: e
An other little moment answered the wife and

tornava a gridare:
(re)turned to shout

"Anna, Anna, sorella mia, non vedi tu apparir
Anna Anna sister (of) mine not see you appear

nessuno?".
no one

"Vedo" ella rispose "due cavalieri che vengono in
(I) see she answered two knights that came in

qua: ma sono ancora molto lontani."
there but (there) are still very far

"Sia ringraziato Iddio", aggiunse un minuto dopo,
Be thankful God (she) added a minute after

"sono proprio i nostri fratelli: io faccio loro
(I) am properly -the- our brothers I make them
(really)

tutti i segni che posso, perché si spiccino
all the signs that (I) can so that themselves (they) hurry

e   arrivino   presto."
and (they) arrive   soon

Intanto   Barba-blu   si   messe   a   gridare   così
Meanwhile   Beard-blue   himself   put   to   yell   so
            (Blue Beard)

forte,   che   fece   tremare   tutta   la   casa.   La
loud   that (she) made tremble   whole the   house   The

povera   donna   ebbe   a   scendere,   e   tutta
poor   woman   had   to   go down   and   all

scapigliata   e   piangente   andò   a   gettarsi
disheveled   and   crying   (she) went to   throw herself

  ai   suoi piedi:
to -the-   his   feet

"Sono   inutili   i   piagnistei",   disse   Barba-blu,
(They) are useless   the   cryings   said   Beard-blue
                             (whining)   (Blue Beard)

 "bisogna   morire".
(you) need to   die

Quindi pigliandola   con   una   mano   per   i   capelli,
When   picking up her with   a   hand   by   the   hairs

e   coll'altra alzando il coltellaccio per   aria,
and with the other lifting the big knife through (the) air

era lì   lì   per   tagliarle   la testa.
was there there for to cut (off) her the head

La   povera donna, voltandosi   verso   di   lui   e
The   poor   woman turning herself towards -of- him and

guardandolo cogli   occhi morenti, gli chiese un
watching   with the eyes   dying   him asked one

ultimo istante per   potersi   raccogliere.
last   moment   for to be able herself to pull together

"No, no!", gridò   l'altro, "raccomandati   subito
No   no   shouted the other recommend yourself immediately

a Dio!", e alzando il braccio...
to God and lifting the   arm

In quel punto fu bussato così forte alla porta di
In that point was knocked so strong at the door of
                                     (loud)

casa,   che Barba-blu   si   arrestò tutt'a un
(the) house that Beard-blue himself stopped all at   a
              (Blue Beard)

tratto; e appena aperto, si videro entrare due
stretch and hardly open oneself saw enter two
(sudden)

cavalieri i quali, sfoderata la spada, si
knights the which unsheathed the sword themselves

gettarono su Barba-blu. Esso li riconobbe
threw on Beard-blue That one there recognized
(Blue beard)

subito per i fratelli di sua moglie, uno
immediately as the brothers of his wife a

dragone e l'altro moschettiere, e per
dragoon and the other musketeer and for

mettersi in salvo, si dette a fuggire. Ma i
to put himself in rescue himself gave to flee But the

due fratelli lo inseguirono tanto a ridosso, che
two brothers him followed so much at behind that

lo raggiunsero prima che potesse arrivare sul
him (they) reached before that (he) could arrive at the

portico di casa. E costì colla spada lo
front porch of (the) house And there with the sword him
{formal use}

passarono da parte a parte e lo lasciarono
(they) passed from side to side and him left

morto. La povera donna era quasi più morta di
dead The poor woman was almost more dead of
(than)

suo marito, e non aveva fiato di rizzarsi per
her husband and not had breath of to raise herself for

andare ad abbracciare i suoi fratelli.
to go to embrace -the- her brothers

E perché Barba-blu non aveva eredi, la moglie
And because Beard-blue not had heirs the wife
(Blue Beard)

sua rimase padrona di tutti i suoi beni: dei
(of) his remained master of all -the- his goods of the

quali, ne dette una parte in dote alla sua
which of it gave one part in dowry to -the- her

sorella Anna, per maritarla con un gentiluomo,
sister Anna for to marry her with a gentleman

col quale da tanto tempo faceva all'amore:
with the which of so much time (she) made to the love

di un'altra se ne servì per comprare il
of an other herself of it (she) served for to buy the

grado di capitano ai suoi fratelli: e il resto lo
grade of captain to the her brothers and the rest it
              (for)

tenne per sé, per maritarsi con un fior di
kept for herself for to marry herself with a flower of

galantuomo, che le fece dimenticare tutti i
(a) gentleman that her made forget all the

crepacuori che aveva sofferto con Barba-blu.
break-hearts that (she) had suffered with Beard-blue
(heartbreaks)   (Blue Beard)

Così per tutti gli sposi.
Like that for all the spouses

Da questo racconto, che risale al tempo delle
From this tale that dates at the time of the
              (from the)

fate, si potrebbe imparare che la
fairies oneself (one) would be able to learn that -the-

curiosità, massime quando è spinta troppo,
curiosity maximum when (it) is thrust too much
     (especially)   (too far)

spesso   e   volentieri   ci   porta   addosso   qualche
often   is   voluntarily   us   carries   on top   some

malanno.
bad-year
(illness)

Enrichetto dal ciuffo

Enrichetto   dal   ciuffo
Little Henry   of the   tuft
(with the)

C'era   una   volta   una   Regina,   la   quale   partorì
There was   one   time   a   Queen   the   which   gave birth to

un   figliuolo   così   brutto   e   così   male   imbastito,   da
a   son   so   ugly   and   so   badly   basted   of
(formed)

far   dubitare   per   un   pezzo   se   avesse   fattezze   di
to make   doubt   for   a   bit   if   (he) had   features   of

bestia   o   di   cristiano.   Una   fata,   che   si   trovò
(a) beast   or   of   (a) christian   A   fairy   that   herself   found
(a human)

presente   al   parto,   dette   per   sicuro   che   egli
present   at the   birth   said   for   sure   that   he

avrebbe   avuto   molto   spirito: e   aggiunse   di   più,
would have   had   much   spirit   and   (she) added   of   more
(wit)

che in grazia di un certo dono particolare,
that in grace of a certain gift particular

fattogli da lei, avrebbe potuto trasfondere
made for him from her (he) would have been able to transform

altrettanta dose di spirito e d'intelligenza in
equally doses of spirit and of intelligence in
(wit)

quella persona, chiunque si fosse, che egli
that person whomever itself was that he

avesse amato sopra tutte le altre.
would have loved over all the others

Questa cosa consolò un poco la povera Regina,
This thing consoled a bit the poor Queen

la quale non poteva darsi pace di aver messo
the which not could give herself peace of to have put

al mondo un brutto marmocchio a quel modo!
into the world an ugly kid at that manner

Il fatto egli è, che appena il fanciullo cominciò
The fact he is that hardly the young boy started

a spiccicar parola, disse delle cose molto
to utter (a) word (he) said of the things very

aggiustate: e in tutto quello che faceva, mostrava
correct and in all that that (he) did (he) showed

un non so che di così aggraziato, che piaceva
a not (I) know what of such grace that pleased

e dava nel genio a tutti. Mi dimenticava di
and gave in the genius to all Myself (I) forgot of

dire che egli nacque con un ciuffettino di capelli
to tell that he was born with a little tuft of hairs
(hair)

sulla testa: e per questo lo chiamarono
on the head and for this him (they) called

Enrichetto dal ciuffo: perché Enrichetto era il
little Henry of the tuft because little Henry was -the-
(with the)

suo nome di battesimo.
his name of baptism

In capo a sette o otto anni, la Regina di uno
In head to seven or eight years the Queen of a
At the end of

Stato vicino partorì due bambine.
state neighboring gave birth to two children

La prima, che venne al mondo, era più
The first that came into the world was more

bella del Sole; e la Regina ne sentì
beautiful of the sun and the Queen of it felt
(than the)

un'allegrezza così grande, da far temere per
a happiness so great of to make fear for

la sua salute.
-the- her health

La stessa fata, che aveva assistito alla nascita di
The same fairy that had assisted to the birth of

Enrichetto dal ciuffo, si trovò presente anche
little Henry of the tuft herself found present also

a quest'altra: e per moderare la gioia della
to this other and for to moderate the joy of the

Regina, le dichiarò che la piccola Principessa
Queen her (she) declared that the little princess

non avrebbe avuto neppur l'ombra dello spirito,
not would have had even the shadow of the spirit
(wit)

per cui sarebbe stata tanto stupida, quanto
for which (she) would be been so stuped as much as
(she would have)

era bella.
(she) was beautiful

La Regina rimase molto male di questa cosa: ma
The Queen remained very bad of this thing but

pochi momenti dopo ebbe un altro dispiacere
little moments after (she) had an other displeasure

anche più grosso, nel vedere che la seconda
also more great in the to see that the second

figlia, che aveva partorito, era talmente brutta da
girl that (she) had given birth to was so ugly of

fare paura.
to make afraid

"Non vi disperate, signora", le disse la fata,
Not yourself get desperate lady her said the fairy

"la vostra figlia sarà ricompensata per un altro
-the- your daughter will be compensated for an other

verso; essa avrà tanto spirito, da non
verse that one will have so much spirit of not
(she) (wit)

avvedersi nemmeno della bellezza che non l'è
to see oneself not even of the beauty that not her is

toccata."
touched
(given)

"Dio voglia che sia così!", rispose la Regina, "ma
God wants that (it) so so answered the Queen but

non ci sarebbe modo di fare avere un po' di
not there would be manner of to make have a bit of

spirito anche alla maggiore che è tanto bella?"
spirit also to the elder that is so beautiful
(wit)

"Per quanto allo spirito, o signora, io non ci
For as much as to the spirit oh lady I not there
(wit)

posso far nulla", disse la fata, "ma posso tutto
can do nothing said the fairy but (I) can everything

per la parte della bellezza; e siccome non c'è
for the part of the beauty and since not there is

cosa al mondo che non farei per vedervi
(a) thing at the world that not would do for to see you

contenta, così le concederò in dono la virtù di
happy so her (I) concede in gift the virtue of

far diventare bella la persona che più
to make become beautiful the person that most

sarà di suo genio."
(she) will of her genius
(liking)

A mano a mano che le due Principesse
At hand to hand that the two Princesses
While gradually

crescevano, crescevano con esse i loro pregi,
grew up grew up with these -the- -their- merits

fino al punto che non si parlava d'altro
until to the point that not oneself talked of other
(people) (of anything else)

che della bellezza della più grande e dello
that of the beauty of the most large and of the
(than) older one

spirito della minore.
spirit   of the younger one
(wit)

È   vero   però   che   anche   i   loro   difetti
(It) is true however that also   -the- their defects

si   facevano   più   vistosi,
themselves   made   more   showy

coll'andare in là degli anni.   La   minore
with the to go in there of the years The   younger
         while they grew older

imbruttiva a occhiate, e   la maggiore diventava
became uglier at eyes   and the elder   became
       became visibly uglier

stupida un giorno più dell'altro, e   non sapeva
dumb   one day more of the other and not knew
       dumber every day

rispondere alle domande che le venivano fatte, o
to respond to the questions that her came   made or
                                        (were)

rispondeva delle sciocchezze. Oltre   a   questo
answered   of the rubbish   Other   at   this
                                       (than)

ell'era così smanierata e   senza garbo   né
she was so   restless   and without politeness nor

grazia, che non era buona di posare quattro
grace that not (she) was good of to set four
(for)

vasi di porcellana sul camminetto senza
vases of porcelain on the little fireplace without

romperne qualcuno, né d'accostarsi alla bocca
to break of them some nor of to set herself to the mouth

un bicchier d'acqua senza versarselo mezzo
a cup of water without to turn itself it half

sul vestito.
over the dress

Sebbene la bellezza sia un gran vantaggio per una
Although the beauty is a great advantage for a

fanciulla, pure è un fatto che la sorella minore
young girl also (it) is a fact that the sister younger

aveva sempre il disopra sull'altra, in società e
had always the advantage over the other in society and

in tutte le conversazioni.
in all the conversations

Sul primo, tutti si voltavano dalla parte
On the first all themselves turned of the part
(At)

della più bella per vederla e ammirarla; ma
of the most beautiful for to see her nad to admire her but

dopo pochi minuti la lasciavano per andare da
after (a) few minutes her (they) left for to go of
(to)

quella che aveva più spirito, a sentire le cose
that one that had more spirit, to hear the things
(intelligence)

graziose che diceva: e faceva maraviglia di
gracious that (she) said and (it) made wonder of

vedere come in meno di un quarto d'ora la
to see how in less of a quarter of (an) hour the
(than)

maggiore non avesse più nessuno dintorno a
elder not had more no one around to
(anyone)

sé, mentre tutti erano a far corona intorno
herself while all were to make crown around

alla sorella minore.
to the sister minor

La maggiore, sebbene molto stupida, si avvide
The older although very dumb herself noticed

di questa cosa: e avrebbe dato volentieri tutta
-of- this thing and would have given voluntarily all

la sua bellezza, per avere la metà dello spirito
-the- her beauty for to have the half of the spirit

della sorella.
of the sister

La Regina, quantunque fosse prudente, non
The Queen although (she) was careful not

seppe stare dallo sgridarla piu volte
knew to stand from -the- to scold her more times
(how to keep) (multiple)

delle sue grullerie: e questa cosa fece tanta
of -the- her stupidities and this thing did so much

pena alla povera Principessa, che si sentì
pain to the poor Princess that herself (she) felt

come morire.
like to die

Un giorno, che era andata nel bosco a
One day that (she) was gone in the forest to

piangere la sua disgrazia, vide venirsi
cry -the- her disgrace (she) saw to come herself

incontro un omiciattolo brutto e spiacente
towards a nasty little fellow ugly and displeasing

quanto mai, ma vestito con grandissima eleganza.
as much ever but dressed with very great elegance

Era il giovane principe Enrichetto dal ciuffo,
(It) was the young prince little Henry of the tuft

il quale innamoratosi di lei al solo vederne
the which in love of her at the only to see of her
(with)

i ritratti che giravano per tutto il
the portraits that made the rounds through all the

mondo, aveva abbandonato il regno di suo padre
world had abandoned the kingdom of his father

per avere il piacere di vederla e di parlarle.
for to have the pleasure of to see her and of to talk to her

Contentissimo di trovarla sola, si avvicinò
Very happy of to find her alone himself (he) approached

a lei con tutto il rispetto e la gentilezza
to her with all the respect and the gentleness

immaginabile. E avendo udito che essa era molto
imaginable And having heard that she was very

afflitta, dopo i soliti complimenti d'uso le
aflicted after the usual compliments of habit her

disse:
(he) said

"Io non so comprendere, o Regina, come
I not know to comprehend oh Queen how

essendo voi così bella come siete, possiate
being you so beautiful as (you) are (you) can

essere triste come apparite; perché, sebbene io
be sad like (you) appear because although I

possa vantarmi di aver veduto un'infinità di
can boast myself of to have seen an infinity of

belle **donne,** **posso** **dire** **di** **non** **averne** **vista**
beautiful women (I) can say of not to have of it seen

una **sola,** **la** **cui** **bellezza** **si** **avvicinasse** **alla**
one alone the whose beauty itself approaches to -the-

vostra".
yours

"A **voi** **piace** **dir** **così!",** **rispose** **la** **Principessa,**
To you (it) pleases to say like that answered the Princess

e **non** **disse** **altro.**
and not said (anything) else

"La **bellezza",** **riprese** **Enrichetto** **dal** **ciuffo,** **"è** **un**
The beauty continued little Henry of the tuft is a

dono **così** **grande,** **che** **deve** **compensare** **di** **tutto**
gift so great that (it) must compensate -of- all

il **resto;** **e** **quando** **la** **si** **possiede,** **non** **vedo**
the rest and when her one possesses not (I) see

nessun'altra **cosa** **che** **possa** **recarci** **afflizione."**
no other thing that can cause itself affliction

"Vorrei",   rispose   la   Principessa,   "essere   brutta
(I) would like   answered   the   Princess   to be   ugly

quanto voi e avere dello spirito; piuttosto che
as much as you and to have of the   spirit   rather   than
                                       (intelligence)

avere   la   bellezza   che   ho,   ed   essere   una
to have   the   beauty   that   (I) have   and   to be   a

stupida come sono."
stupid girl   like   (I) am

"Non c'è nulla, o signora, che dia segno di aver
Not   it is nothing   oh   lady   that   gives   sign   of   to have

dello spirito,   quanto   il   credere di non averne:
of the   spirit   as much as   the   believe   of   not   to have it
         (wit)

egli è uno di quei pregi, che per la sua indole
it   is   one   of   those   merits   that   for   the   its   indolent

singolare, più se ne ha, e più si crede di
particularity   more   one   of it   has   and   more   one   believes   of

esserne mancanti."
to be of it   lacking

"Io non m'intendo di queste cose", disse la
I not myself understand of these things said the

Principessa, "ma so benissimo che io sono una
Princess but (I) know very well that I am a

grande imbecille, ed ecco la cagione del dolore,
great imbecile and here the cause of the pain

che mi farà morire."
that me will make die

"Se non è che questo che vi tormenta, o
If not is that this what you torments oh
(more than)

signora, io posso facilmente metter fine alla
lady I can easily put end to -the-

vostra afflizione."
your affliction

"E come fare?", disse la Principessa,
And how to do said the Princess

"Io ho il potere", disse Enrichetto dal ciuffo, "di
I have the power said little Henry of the tuft of

trasfondere tutto lo spirito, che può desiderarsi,
to instill / all / the / spirit / that / can / to desire oneself
(wit)

in quella persona che io dovrò amare sopra le
in / that / person / that / I / will have to / love / over / the

altre; e siccome voi siete quella, così dipende da
others / and / since / you / are / that / like so / depends / of

voi di possedere tanto spirito, quanto se ne
you / of / to possess / so much / spirit / as much as / yourself / of it
(wit)

può avere, solo che siate contenta di
can / have / only / that / (you) are / happy / of
(as long as)

sposarmi."
to marry me

La Principessa rimase come una statua, e non
The / Princess / remained / like / a / statue / and / not

rispose sillaba.
answered / (a) syllable

"Vedo bene", rispose Enrichetto dal ciuffo, "che
(I) see / well / answered / little Henry / of the / tuft / that

questa mia proposta non vi è andata punto a
-this- my proposal not you is gone point to

genio: e non me ne faccio nessuna meraviglia;
genius and not me of it (I) make none wonder
(any) (surprise)

ma vi lascio un anno intero, perché possiate
but you (I) let a year entire so that (you) can
(I give)

prendere una risoluzione."
take a decision

La Principessa aveva così poco spirito, e al
The Princess had such little spirit and at the
(intelligence)

tempo stesso sentiva tanta voglia di averne, che
time same felt so much want of to have it that

s'immaginò che la fine dell'anno non sarebbe
(she) herself imagined that the end of the year not would be
(would have)

arrivata mai, e così accettò la proposizione che
arrived ever and so accepted the proposition that

le veniva fatta.
her came made
(was)

Appena ebbe promesso a Enrichetto dal ciuffo
Hardly had (she) promised to little Henry of the tuft

che dentro un anno e in quello stesso giorno
that inside a year and in that same day
(who)

l'avrebbe sposato, si sentì subito molto
her would have married herself (she) felt immediately very

diversa da quella di prima; e provò una
different from that of first and (she) experienced an

facilità incredibile a dire tutte le cose che
ease incredible to say all the things that

voleva dire, e a dirle in un modo grazioso,
(she) wanted to say and to say them in a manner gracious

spontaneo e naturale. Cominciò da questo
spontaneous and natural (She) began from this

momento a metter su una conversazione elegante
moment to put on a conversation elegant

e ben condotta con Enrichetto dal ciuffo, nella
and well led with little Henry of the tuft in the

quale essa brillò con tanta vivacità, che a
which that one shone with so much liveliness that to

questi nacque il dubbio di averle dato più
this one gave birth the doubt of to have her given more

spirito di quello che se ne fosse serbato per
spirit of that what itself of it was retained for
(wit)

sé.
himself

Ritornata che fu al palazzo, la Corte non
Returned that was to the palace the Court not

sapeva che pensare di un cambiamento così
knew what to think of a change so

improvviso e straordinario; dappoiché, per quante
sudden and extraordinary from then on for as many

sguaiataggini le avevano udito dire in passato, ora
coarsenesses her (they) had heard say in (the) past now

la sentivano dire altrettante cose spiritosissime e
her heard say many things very witty and

piene   di   buon   senso.
full   of   good   sense

Tutta   la   Corte   n'ebbe   un'allegrezza   tale   da   non
Whole   the Court   of it had a happiness   such   of   not

figurarselo.   Non   ci   fu   la   sorella   minore,
to imagine oneself it Not   there was   the   sister   minor

che   non   ne   restasse   contenta,   perché   non   avendo
that   not   of it remained   happy   because   not   having

più   sulla   maggiore   il   disopra   dello   spirito,   faceva
more   on the   elder   the   of over   of the   spirit   made
                                                    (wit)

ora   accanto   a   lei   la   figura   meschinissima   d'una
now   together   to   her   the   figure   wretched   of a

bertuccia.
barbary ape

Il   Re   si   lasciava   guidare   da   lei,   e   qualche
The   King   himself   let   guide   by   her   and   some

volta   andava   fino   a   tener   consiglio   nel   suo
time   went   until   to   keep   council   in -the-   her

quartiere.
quarter

La diceria di questo cambiamento essendosi sparsa
The saying of this change being itself spread

all'intorno, tutti i giovani principi degli Stati
to the around all the young princes of the State

vicini fecero a gara per arrivare a
neighboring made -to- competition for to arrive to

farsi amare, e quasi tutti la chiesero in
make themselves to love and almost all her asked in
(be loved)

sposa ma essa non trovava chi avesse abbastanza
spouse but she not found who had enough
(marriage)

spirito, e faceva lo stesso viso a tutte le
spirit and made the same face to all the
(wit) (reaction)

offerte di matrimonio, senza impegnarsi con
offers of matrimony without to commit herself with

alcuno.
any

Intanto   se   ne presentò uno così potente, così
Meanwhile itself of it presented one so potent so

ricco, e così spiritoso e bello della persona,
rich and so spirited and beautiful of the person

che ella non poté stare dal sentire una certa
that she not could be of the to feel a certain

inclinazione per lui.
inclination for him

Suo padre, che se n'era avveduto, le disse che
His father that itself of it was circumspect her said that

la lasciava padrona di scegliersi lo sposo a
her (he) left master of to choose herself the spouse at

modo suo, e che non aveva da far altro che
manner hers and that not to have of to make else than

far conoscere la sua volontà.
to make to know -the- her wish

E siccome accade che più uno ha dello
And since (it) happened that more one has of the

spirito, e più si trova impensierito a pigliare
spirit (wit) — and — more — one — finds — thoughtful — and — to take

una risoluzione stabile in certe faccende, essa,
a — resolution — stable — in — certain — matters — she

dopo aver ringraziato suo padre, domandò che le
after — to have — thanked — her — father — asked — that — her

fosse dato un po' di tempo per poterci
was — given — a — little — -of- — time — for — to be able there

pensar sopra.
to think — over

E per caso andò a passeggiare in quel bosco
And — by — case (chance) — (she) went — to — pass — in — that — forest

dove aveva incontrato Enrichetto dal ciuffo, per
where — (she) had — encountered — little Henry — of the — tuft — for

avere il modo di pensare comodamente alla
to have — the — manner — of — to think — comfortably — to the

risoluzione da prendere.
resolutions — of — to take

Mentr'ella   passeggiava   tutt'immersa   ne'   suoi
While she   passed   all immersed   in -the-   her

pensieri sentì sotto i piedi un rumore sordo,
thoughts (she) felt under the feet a sound mute

come di molte persone che vadano e vengano,
like of many persons that went and came

e si dieno un gran da fare.
and themselves gave a great of to do

Avendo teso l'orecchio con più attenzione,
Having strained the ear with more attention

sentì qualcuno che diceva: "Passami codesta
(she) heard someone that said Pass me that

caldaia"; e un altro: "Metti della legna sul
cauldron and an other Put of the wood on the

fuoco".
fire

La terra si aprì in quel momento, ed ella
The ground itself opened in that moment and she

vide sotto i suoi piedi come una gran cucina
saw under -the- her feet like a great kitchen

piena di cuochi, di sguatteri e d'ogni sorta di
filled of cooks of scullions and of each kind of

gente necessaria per allestire una gran festa. E
people necessary for prepare a great feast And

di lì uscì fuori una schiera di venti o trenta
from there exited outside a host of twenty or thirty

rosticcieri, che andarono a piantarsi in un
caterers that went to plant themselves in an

viale del bosco, intorno a una lunghissima
avenue of the forest around at a very long

tavola, e tutti colla ghiotta in mano e colla
table and all with the greedy in hand and with the

coda di volpe sull'orecchio si posero a
tail of foxes on the ear themselves put to

lavorare a tempo di musica, sul motivo di una
work at time of music on the motive of a
(the rhythm)

graziosa canzone.
pretty   song

La   Principessa,   stupita   di   quello   spettacolo,
The   Princess   shocked   of   that   spectacle

domandò loro per chi fossero in tanto lavorìo.
asked   them for who (they) were in so much   work

"Lavoriamo", rispose il capoccia della brigata, "per
(We) work   answered the ringleaders of the   brigade   for

il   signor Enrichetto   dal   ciuffo, che domani è
the   Mr.   little Henry   of the   tuft   that tomorrow is

sposo."
spouse
(married)

La   Principessa,   sempre   più   meravigliata,   e
The   Princess   always   more   surprised   and

ricordandosi   a   un   tratto che un anno fa,
remembering herself at (all of) a   tract   that   a   year ago
                               (sudden)

e in quello stesso giorno, aveva promesso di
and in   that   same   day   had   promised of

sposare il principe Enrichetto dal ciuffo, credé
to marry the prince little Henry of the tuft believed

di cascare dalle nuvole. La ragione della sua
of to fall from the cloud The reason of -the- his

dimenticanza stava in questo che, quando
forgetfulness stood in this that when

promise, era sempre la solita stupida, e
(she) promised (she) was always the usual dumb girl and
(still)

acquistando in seguito lo spirito che il Principe
acquiring in following the spirit that the Prince
(wit)

le aveva dato, non si ricordava più di
her had given not herself remembered (any)more of

tutte le sue grullerie.
all the her nonsense

Non aveva fatto ancora trenta passi, seguitando
Not (she) had made still thirty paces continuing

la sua passeggiata, che s'imbatté in
-the- her walk that (she) stumbled into in
(than)

Enrichetto   dal   ciuffo,   il   quale   si   faceva
little Henry   of the   tuft   the   which   himself   made

avanti   tutto   sgargiante   e   magnifico,   come   un
ahead   all   showy   and   magnificent   like   a

Principe   che   vada   a   nozze.
Prince   that   goes   to   marriage

"Eccomi   qui,   signora",   egli   disse,   "puntuale   alla
Here me   here   lady   he   said   punctual   at -the-
(See me)

mia   parola: e   non   ho   il   minimo   dubbio   che
my   word   and   not   (I) have   the   least   doubt   that

voi   siate   venuta   qui   per   mantenere   la   vostra,   e
you   are   come   here   for   to maintain   the   your   and
(have)

per   far   di   me,   col   dono   della   vostra   mano,
for   to make   of   me   with the   gift   of the   your   hand

il   mortale   più   felice   di   questa   terra."
the   mortal   most   happy   of   this   earth

"Vi   confesserò   francamente",   rispose   la
You   (I) will confess   honestly   answered   the

Principessa, "che su questa cosa non ho presa
Princess · that · on · this · case · not · (I) have · taken

ancora nessuna risoluzione; e ho paura che, se
yet · no · decision · and · (I) have · fear · that · if

dovrò prenderne una, non sarà mai quella che
(I) will have · to take of it · one · not · (I) will · ever · that · what

desiderate."
(you) desire

"Voi mi fate stupire, o signora", disse Enrichetto
You · me · make · astound · oh · lady · said · little Henry

dal ciuffo.
of the · tuft

"Lo capisco", disse la Principessa, "difatti mi
It · (I) understand · said · the · Princess · of facts · me
(in fact)

troverei in un grandissimo impiccio, se avessi da
(I) would find · in · a · great · mess · if · (I) had · of

fare con un uomo brutale e senza spirito. Una
to do · with · a · man · brutal · and · without · wit · A

Principessa **mi** **ha** **dato** **la** **sua** **parola,** **egli** **mi**
Princess me has given -the- her word he me

direbbe; **e** **una volta** **che** **mi** **ha** **promesso,**
would say and one time that me (she) has promised
once

bisogna **bene** **che** **mi** **sposi.** **Ma** **poiché** **la**
(it) is necessary well that me (he) marries But since the

persona **colla** **quale** **parlo,** **è** **la** **persona** **più**
person with the which (I) talk is the person most

spiritosa **di** **questo** **mondo,** **così** **sono** **sicura** **che**
spirited of this world so (I) am sure that
(intelligent)

vorrà **capacitarsi** **della** **ragione.** **Voi**
(he) will want to comprehend himself -of- the reason You
(to understand)

sapete **che** **anche** **allora,** **quand'ero** **stupida,** **non**
know that also then when (I) am stupid not

sapevo **risolvermi** **a** **doversi** **sposare;** **e** **vi**
(I) know to resolve myself to must himself marry and you

par **egli** **possibile** **che** **ora,** **dopo** **tutto** **lo** **spirito**
seem him possible that now after all the spirit
(wit)

che mi avete dato, e che mi ha resa di più
that me (you) have given and that me has yielded of more

difficile contentatura, di quel che fossi prima,
difficult contentment of that what (I) was first

possa oggi prendere una risoluzione che non
(that I) can today take a decision that not

sono stata buona di prendere per il passato? Se
(I) am been good of to take for the past If
(I have) (in)

vi premeva tanto di sposarmi, avete avuto un
you pressed so much of to marry me (you) have had a
(made)

gran torto a togliermi dalla mia stupidaggine,
great mistake to rid me of -the- my stupidities

e a farmi aprire gli occhi, perché ci vedessi
and to make me open the eyes because you see

meglio d'una volta."
better of one time
(than one)

"Se un uomo senza spirito", rispose Enrichetto
If a man without spirit answered little Henry
(wit)

dal   ciuffo, "sarebbe ben accolto, stando a quello
of the   tuft   would be   well   received   standing at   that

che   dite,   quando venisse a rinfacciarvi la parola
what (you) say   when   comes   to reproach you the   word

mancata, o perché volete che io non   debba
failed   or   maybe (you) want that I   not would have to

valermi degli stessi mezzi, per una cosa nella
value me of the   same   places   for   one   thing in -the-

quale è riposta la felicità di tutta   la   mia vita?
which is posed   the happiness of   all   -the- my   life

Vi pare egli ragionevole che le persone di spirito
You seem it   reasonable   that the persons of   spirit
                                                                               (wit)

debbano   trovarsi   in   peggiore condizione   di
should   find himself in   worse   conditions   of
                                                                               (than)

quelle che non ne hanno? E potete pretenderlo
those that not of it have And can   pretend it

voi? voi che ne avete tanto e che avete
you you that of it have so much and that (you) have

tanto desiderato di averne? Ma veniamo al
so much desired   of to have of it But (we) came at the

sodo, se vi contentate. All'infuori della
hard (kernel) if you content yourself At the outwards from -the-
                                           (Apart)

mia bruttezza, c'è forse in me qualche cosa che
my ugliness it is maybe in me some thing that
              (is there)

vi dispiaccia? Siete forse scontenta della mia
you displeases (You) are maybe discontent of -the- my

nascita, del mio spirito, del mio carattere,
birth of -the- my spirit of -the- my character

delle mie maniere?"
of -the- my manners

"Tutt'altro", rispose la Principessa, "anzi, tutte le
All else answered the Princess also all the

cose che avete nominate, sono appunto quelle
things that (you) have named are exactly that

che mi piacciono in voi."
what me (they) please in you

"Quand'è così", rispose Enrichetto dal ciuffo,
When (it) is so answered little Henry of the tuft

"sono felice, perché non sta che a voi a fare di
(I) am happy because not (it) is that to you to make of
(but)

me il più bello e il più grazioso degli
me the most beautiful and the most gracious of the

uomini."
men

"Ma come può accader questo?", chiese la
But how can happen this answered the

Principessa.
Princess

"Il come è facile", rispose Enrichetto dal ciuffo.
The how is easy answered little Henry of the tuft

"Basta che voi mi amiate tanto, da desiderare
(It) is enough that you me love so much of to desire

che ciò accada: e perché, o signora, non vi
that what happens and because oh lady not you

nasca   dubbio su quello che dico, sappiate che
give birth to doubt on that what (I) say (you) know that
(have)

la medesima fata, che nel giorno della mia
the same fairy that in the day of -the- my

nascita mi fece il dono di rendere spiritosa la
birth me made the gift of to render spirited the
(intelligent)

persona che più mi fosse piaciuta, diede a voi
person that most me makes pleased gave to you

pure quello di far diventare bello colui che
also that of to make become beautiful him that

amerete, e al quale vorrete far di genio
(you) love and at the which (you) want to make of genius
(liking)

e volentieri questo favore."
and voluntarily this favor

"Se la cosa sta come la raccontate", disse la
If the thing is like it (you) tell said the
(how)

Principessa, "vi desidero con tutto il cuore che
Princess you (I) desire with all the heart that

diventiate il Principe più simpatico e più
(you) become the Prince most sympathetic and most

bello del mondo, e per quanto è da me, ve
beautiful of the world and for as much is of me you

ne faccio pienissimo dono."
of it (I) make (the) fullest gift

La Principessa aveva appena finito di dire queste
The Princess had hardly finished of to say these

parole, che subito Enrichetto dal ciuffo
words that immediately little Henry of the tuft

apparve ai suoi occhi il più bell'uomo della
appeared at -the- her eyes the most beautiful man of the

terra, e il meglio formato, e il più amabile
earth and the best formed and the most amiable
                                    (educated)

di quanti se ne fossero mai veduti.
of so much self of it were ever seen

Vogliono alcuni che questo cambiamento avvenisse
Want some that this change happened
Some say

non già per gl'incanti della fata, ma
not already because of the enchantments of the fairy but

unicamente per merito dell'amore. E dicono che
only for merit of the love And (they) said that

la Principessa, avendo ripensato meglio alla
the Princess having thought again better at the

costanza del suo cuore e della sua mente,
constancy of -the- her heart and of -the- her mind

non vide più le deformità personali di lui,
not (he) saw (any)more the deformedness personal of him

né la bruttezza del suo viso: talché il
nor the ugliness of -the- his face so that the

gobbo che egli aveva di dietro, le sembrò quella
hunchback that he had of back her seemed that

specie di rotondità e di floridezza d'aspetto di
sort of rotundness and of floridity of aspect of

chi dà nell'ingrassare: e invece di vederlo
who gives in the fattening and instead of to see him

zoppicare orribilmente, come aveva fatto fino
to limp   horribly   like   (he) had made until

allora, le parve che avesse un'andatura
then   her (it) seemed that (he) had   a walk

aggraziata e un po' buttata su una parte, che le
gracious and a bit thrown on one side that her

piaceva moltissimo. Fu detto fra le altre
pleased very much (It) was said between the other

cose, che gli occhi di lui, che erano guerci, le
things that the eyes of him that were squinting her

parvero più brillanti; e che finisse col
seemed more brilliant and that (she) finished with the

mettersi in testa che quel modo storto di
to set himself in head that that manner distorted of

guardare fosse il segno di un violento accesso di
to watch was the sign of a violent access of

amore: e che perfino il naso di lui, grosso e
love and that even the nose of him large and

rosso come un peperone, accennasse a qualche
red like a pepper alluded at some

cosa di serio e di marziale.
thing of serious and of martial
(military)

Fatto sta che la Principessa gli promise, lì
Fact is that the Princess him promised there

sul tamburo, che l'avrebbe sposato, purché
on the drum that him she would have married provided

ne avesse ottenuto il consenso dal Re suo
of it (she) had obtained the consent of the King her

padre.
father

Il Re, avendo saputo che la sua figlia aveva
The King having known that -the- his daughter had

moltissima stima per Enrichetto dal ciuffo, che
very much esteem for little Henry of the tuft that

egli del resto conosceva per un Principe
he of the rest knew for a Prince

spiritosissimo e pieno di giudizio, lo accettò con
very spirited — and — full — of judgement — him — accepted — with

piacere per suo genero.
pleasure — as — his — son-in-law

Il giorno dipoi furono fatte le nozze, come
The — day — afterwards — were — made — the — nuptials — as
was arranged the wedding

Enrichetto dal ciuffo aveva preveduto, e a
little Henry — of the — tuft — had — expected — and — at

seconda degli ordini che egli medesimo aveva
second — of the — orders — that — he — very same — had
(himself)

già dato da molto tempo prima.
already — given — of — very — time — before

Questa sembrerebbe una favola; eppure è una
This — would seem — a — fable — but yet — (it) is — a

storia. Tutto ci par bello nella persona
story — All — to us — seems — beautiful — in the — person

amata, anche i difetti: tutto ci par grazioso,
loved — also — the — defects — all — to us — seems — gracious
(that we love)

anche le sguaiataggini.
also the vulgarities

La storia d'Enrichetto dal ciuffo è vecchia quanto
The story of little Henry of the tuft is old as

il mondo.
the world

La Bella dai capelli d' oro

La Bella dai   capelli d' oro
The Beauty of the   hairs   of gold
        with the golden hair

C'era   una volta la   figlia di un Re, la quale
There was one time the daughter of a king the which
                           who

era tanto bella, che in tutto il mondo non si
was so   beautiful that in all the world not itself

dava l'eguale; e per cagione di questa sua grande
gave the equal and for cause of -this- her great

bellezza,   la   chiamavano   la   Bella
beauty   her   (they) called   the   Beauty

dai capelli d'oro, perché i   suoi capelli erano
of the hairs of gold because -the- her hairs were
with the golden hair

più fini dell'oro,   e   biondi   e   pettinati   a
more fine of the gold and blond   and   combed   at
more beautiful than gold

meraviglia le scendevano giù fino ai piedi.
wonder her went down down until to the feet

Essa andava sempre coperta dai suoi capelli
She went always covered of the her hairs
(with)

inanellati, con in capo una ghirlanda di fiori
ringed with in head a garland of flowers
(curled) (on the)

e con delle vesti tutte tempestate di diamanti
and with -of the- dresses all studded of diamonds
(with)

e di perle, tanto che era impossibile
and of pearls so much that (it) was impossible
(with)

vederla e non restarne invaghiti.
to look at her and not to remain of it enamored

In quelle vicinanze c'era un giovane Re,
In those neighborhoods there was a young king
(

il quale non aveva moglie, ed era molto ricco
the which not had (a) wife and (who) was very rich
who

e molto bello della persona.
and very handsome of the person
(had very) looks

Quando egli venne a sapere tutte le belle cose
When he came to know all the beautiful things

che si dicevano della Bella
that themselves said of the Beauty
(people)

dai capelli d'oro,   sebbene
of the hairs of gold   even if
with the golden hair

non l'avesse ancora veduta, se ne innamorò
not her had still seen himself with her fell in love
he had not seen her yet

così forte, che non beveva né mangiava più;
so strongly that not (he) drank nor (he) ate (any)more

finché un bel giorno, fatto animo risoluto,
until one beautiful day made (up) (the) mind resolutely

pensò di mandare un ambasciatore per
(he) thought of to send an ambassador for

chiederla in isposa.
to ask her in spouse
(marriage)

Fece fabbricare apposta una magnifica carrozza
(He) let make especially a magnificent carriage

per il suo ambasciatore: gli dette più di
for the his ambassador him (he) gave more of
(than)

cento cavalli e cento servitori, e si
(a) hundred horses and (a) hundred servants and himself

raccomandò a più non posso perché gli
recommended to most not (he) could for that him
as much as possible

conducesse la Principessa.
(he) lead the princess
(he would bring back)

Appena l'ambasciatore ebbe preso congedo dal
Hardly the ambassador had taken leave of the

Re e si fu messo in viaggio, alla Corte
king and himself was set in journey at the court
(on his)

non si parlava d'altro: e il Re, che
not themselves talked of other and the king that
(people) (of anything else)

non dubitava punto che la Principessa non
not doubted at all that the princess not

volesse acconsentire ai suoi desideri,
wanted to consent to -the- his desires
(would want)

cominciò subito a farle allestire degli
began immediately to make for her prepare -of the-

abiti bellissimi e dei mobili di gran valore.
dresses most beautiful and -of the- furniture of great value

Intanto che erano dietro a questi preparativi,
Meanwhile that were behind to these preparations

l'ambasciatore, che era arrivato alla Corte della
the ambassador that was arrived at the court of the
(had

Bella dai capelli d'oro, recitò il suo bravo
Beauty of the hairs of gold recited -the- his good
with the golden hair

discorso; ma sia che la Principessa in quel
speech but whether that the princess in that

giorno non fosse di buon umore, sia che il
day not was of good mood (or) whether that the

complimento non le andasse a genio, fatto sta
compliment not her went to gift fact is
suited

che rispose all'ambasciatore di ringraziare il
that (she) answered -to- the ambassador of to thank the

Re e di dirgli che non aveva voglia di
king and of to tell him that not (she) had will of
(desire)

maritarsi.
to marry herself

L'ambasciarore se ne partì dalla Principessa
The ambassador himself of it left from the princess

dispiacentissimo di non poterla condur seco:
most hunhappy of not to be able her to lead with him
(to bring) {him-with}

e riportò indietro tutti i regali, che doveva
and (he) brought back all the presents that (he) had to

presentarle da parte del Re: perché la
present her from part of the king because the

Principessa era molto onesta, e sapeva che alle
princess was very honest and knew that to the

ragazze non sta bene di accettare i regali
girls not (it) was good of to accept the gifts

dai giovinotti.
from the young men

Per cui non volle gradire né i diamanti
For which not (she) wanted to accept neither the diamonds

né le altre cose; e solo per non scontentare il
nor the other things and only for not to displease the

Re, accettò una carta di spilli d'Inghilterra.
king (she) accepted a card of pins of England

Quando l'ambasciatore fu tornato alla capitale
When the ambassador was returned to the capital
(had)

dove il suo Re lo aspettava con tanta
where -the- his king him awated with so much

impazienza, tutti rimasero male dal vedere
impatience all remained (feeling) bad from the to see

che non avesse condotto seco la Principessa,
that not (he) had brought with him the princess

e il Re si messe a piangere come un
and the king himself set to cry like a

ragazzo, né c'era verso di consolarlo.
boy nor there was verse of to console him

Si trovava lì, alla Corte, un giovinetto
Itself (was) found there at the court a young man

bello come il sole, il più grazioso di tutti gli
handsome like the sun the most gracious of all the

abitanti del Regno. A cagione appunto delle
inhabitants of the kingdom At cause exactly of -the-

sue belle maniere e del suo spirito, lo
his nice manners and of -the- his spirit him

chiamavano "Avvenente".
(they) called Comely

Tutti gli volevano bene, meno gli invidiosi, che
All him wished well less the jealous (ones) that

si rodevano dalla rabbia perché il Re lo
themselves raged from the anger because the king him

colmava di favori e lo metteva a parte d'ogni
filled of favors and him set to side of each
(with) made part

suo segreto.
his secret

Accade che Avvenente si trovò in un
(It) happened that Comely himself found in a

crocchio di persone, che parlavano del ritorno
group of people that talked of the return

dell'ambasciatore e dicevano che non era stato
of the ambassador and said that not was been
(it had)

buono a nulla; allora egli disse, senza badarci
good for nothing then he said without mind it

tanto né quanto:
so much nor how much

"Se il Re avesse mandato me dalla Bella dai
If the king had sent me of the Beauty of the
(to)

capelli d'oro, son sicuro che ella sarebbe venuta
hairs of gold (I) am sure that she would be come
(would have)

meco".
with me

Senza metter tempo in mezzo quei malanni
Without to put time in half those miserables
Without waiting

risoffiarono subito queste parole al Re e
rebreathed immediately these words to the king and

gli dissero:
him said

"Sapete, o Sire, che cosa ha detto Avvenente?
(You) know oh Sire what thing has said Comely

ha detto che se aveste mandato lui dalla Bella
(he) has said that if (you) had sent him of the Beauty
(to)

dai capelli d'oro, egli si riprometteva di
of the hairs of gold he himself promised of

condurla seco. Vedete quant'è maligno! e'
to lead her with him See how (he) is malicious and

pretende di essere più bello di voi, e
pretends of to be more beautiful of you and
(than)

vorrebbe dare ad intendere che la Principessa
would like to give to understand that the Princess

si sarebbe tanto invaghita di lui, da seguitarlo
herself would be so much enamored of him of to follow him

da per tutto".
of for all

Ecco il Re che va in bestia e si riscalda
See the king that went in beast and himself heated

in modo da perdere il lume degli occhi: "Ah! ah!",
in manner of to lose the light of the eyes Ah ah

egli dice, "dunque questo bel mugherino si
he said So this handsome jasmine flower himself
{dandy}

piglia giuoco della mia disgrazia? dunque si
catches game of -the- my disgrace so himself

stima da più di me? Olà: mettetelo
(he) estimates of more of me Oi put him
(than)

subito nella gran torre, e che lì ci muoia
immediately in the large tower and that there he dies

di fame".
of hunger

Le guardie del Re andarono da Avvenente, il
The guards of the king went of Comely the
(for)

quale non si ricordava nemmeno di quello che
who not himself remembered even of that what

aveva detto: lo trascinarono in prigione e gli
(he) had said him (they) dragged in prison and him

fecero mille angherie.
made (a) thousand harassments

Questo povero giovine non aveva che un po' di
This poor young man not had that one bit of
(but)

paglia a uso di letto: e certo vi sarebbe
straw to use of bed and certainly there would be
(as) (he would have)

morto, senza una piccola fontana, che scaturiva a
died without a little fountain that flowed at

piè della torre, dove egli pigliava qualche sorso
(the) foot of the tower where he took some sip

d'acqua per rinfrescarsi un poco, perché la
of water for to refresh himself a bit because the

fame gli aveva seccata la gola.
hunger him had dried the throat

Un   giorno,   non   potendone   più,   diceva
One   day   not   being able   (any) more   (he) said

sospirando:
  sighing

"Di che mai   si   lamenta il Re?   Fra   tutti   i
Of what ever himself complains the king Between all the

suoi sudditi non   ce   n'è   uno che, quanto   me,
his   subjects not there not is one that as much as me

gli sia fedele. Non   ho   ricordanza di   averlo
him   is   faithful Not (I) have   memory   of   to have him

offeso mai!".
offended   ever

Il   Re, per caso, passando vicino alla torre, sentì
The king by   case   passing   close to the tower heard
                (chance)

 i   lamenti di   colui   che aveva   tanto   amato,
the lamentations of that one that (he) had so much loved

e   si   fermò per stare in orecchio: quantunque
and himself stopped for to be in   ear   although
                             to listen

i	cortigiani,	che	erano	con	lui,	e	che
the	cortiers	that	were	with	him	and	that

l'avevano	a	morte	con	Avvenente,	dicessero	al
it had hated	to	death	with	Comely	said	to the

Re: "Che	idea	è	la	vostra,	o	Sire?	non	sapete
king What	idea	is	the	yours	oh	sire	not	know (do you know)

che	è	un	malanno?".	E	il	Re	rispose:
that	(he) is	a	disease	And	the	king	answered

"Lasciatemi	qui:	voglio	sentire	quello	che	dice".
let me	here	(I) want	to hear	that	what	(he) says

E	avendo	sentito	i	lamenti	di	lui,	gli	occhi	gli
And	having	heard	the	laments	of	him	the	eyes	him

s'empirono	di	pianto:	aprì	la	porta	della
themselves filled	of	crying	(he) opened	the	door	of the

torre,	e	lo	chiamò.
tower	and	him	called

Avvenente,	tutto	desolato,	andò	a	buttarsi	ai
Comely	all	desolate	went	to	throw himself	to the

ginocchi del Re, e gli baciò i piedi. "Che cosa
knees of the king and him kissed the feet What thing

v'ho fatto, o Sire", egli disse, "per meritarmi
you (I) have done oh sire he said for to merit me

sì duri trattamenti?"
such harsh treatments

"Tu ti sei preso giuoco di me e del mio
You yourself are taken game of me and of -the- my

ambasciatore", rispose il Re, "tu ti sei lasciato
ambassador answered the king you yourself are let

uscir di bocca che, se avessi mandato te dalla
exit of mouth that if (I) had send you of the
(to)

Bella dai capelli d'oro, ti saresti stimato
Beauty of the hairs of gold yourself (you) would be esteemed
(would have)

da tanto da menarla teco."
from so much of to take her with you
(as)

"È vero, Sire", disse Avvenente, "io le avrei
(It) is true sire said Comely I her would have

raccontato così bene le vostre virtù e i
told so well -the- your virtues and -the-

vostri pregi, che son sicuro che ella non avrebbe
your merits that (I) am sure that she not would have

saputo come resistere; e in tutto questo non mi
known how to resist and in all this not me

par che ci sia cosa che possa offendervi."
seems that there is (a) thing that could offend you

Il Re riconobbe, difatto, di aver torto: dette
The king recognizes of fact of to have wrong (he) gave
(admitted) (in fact) (to be)

un'occhiata a coloro, che gli avevano messo in
a glance at those that him had put in

disgrazia il suo favorito, e lo menò con sé,
disgrace -the- his favorite and him took with himself

non senza pentirsi amaramente del gran
not without to repent himself bitterly of the great

dispiacere che gli aveva dato.
displeasure that him (he) had given
(unpleasantness)

Dopo averlo invitato a una lauta cena, lo
After of to have him invited at a lavish dinner him

chiamò nel suo gabinetto e gli disse:
called in -the- his cabinet and him said

"Avvenente, io amo sempre la Bella dai capelli
Comely I love always -the- Beauty of the hairs
(still)

d'oro; il suo rifiuto non mi ha levato di
of gold -the- her refusal not me has lifted of
(undid)

speranza, ma non so che strada mi prendere
hope but not (I) know what road myself to take

per indurla a diventare mia sposa. Ho una
for to induce her to become my bride (I) have a

gran voglia di mandar te, per vedere se tu
great desire of to send you for to see whether you

fossi buono di venirne a capo".
were good of to come with it to head

Avvenente rispose che era dispostissimo a
Comely answered that (he) was very disposed to

obbedirlo in ogni cosa, e che sarebbe partito
obey him in each thing and that would be left
(he would have)

subito, anche l'indomani.
immediately even the next day

"Oh!", disse il Re, "ti voglio dare una splendida
Oh said the king you (I) want to give a splendid

accompagnatura..."
accompaniment
(escort)

"Non mi par punto necessaria", egli rispose,
Not me (it) seems at all necessary he answered

"quanto a me, mi basta e me n'avanza
(in) as much to me me (it is) enough and me of it advance
(give)

d'un bel cavallo e di qualche lettera da poter
-of- a beautiful horse and of some letters to be able

presentare da parte vostra."
to present from part yours

Il Re non poté stare dall'abbracciarlo per la
The king not could stand of the to embrace him for the
(stop) (of embracing him)

gran   **contentezza**   **di**   **vederlo**   **così**   **pronto**   **e**
great   happiness   of   to see him   so   ready   and

sollecito a partire.
prompt   to   leave

Egli prese congedo dal Re e dai suoi amici
He   took   leave   of the   king   and   of -the-   his   friends

un lunedì mattina, e si pose in viaggio per
a   Monday   morning   and   himself   set   in   journey   for

compiere la sua ambasciata da sé solo, senza
to fulfill   -the-   his   embassy   by   himself   alone   without

fare vistosità e senza fracasso.
to make   splash   and   without   noise

Lungo la strada non faceva altro che studiare
Along   the   road   not   (he) did   other   that   to study
                                            (anything) (than)

tutti i modi per impegnare la Bella dai capelli
all   the   ways   for   to engage   the   Beauty   of the   hairs

d'oro a divenire la sposa del Re. Portava in
of gold   to   become   the   spouse   of the   king   (He) carried   in

tasca un piccolo calamaio, e quando gli veniva
(a) bag a small ink-pot and when him came

qualche bel pensierino da incastrare nel suo
some beautiful thought of to fit in -the- his

discorso, scendeva da cavallo e si
speech (he) dismounted from (his) horse and himself

metteva sotto un albero per pigliarne ricordo
set under a tree for to catch of it (the) memory

prima che gli passasse dalla memoria.
before that him (it) passed from the memory

Una mattina, che era partito sul far del
One morning that (he) was left on the to make of the

giorno, passando da una gran prateria, gli venne
day passing by a large prairy him came

in mente un'idea gentile e graziosa; e
in mind an idea gentle and gracious and

sceso subito di sella, andò a
(he) discended immediately from (the) saddle went to

mettersi **sotto** **una** **sfilata** **di** **salici** **e** **di** **pioppi,**
put himself · under · a · row · of · willows · and · of · poplars

piantati **lungo** **un** **piccolo** **ruscello** **che** **scorreva**
planted · along · a · small · stream · that · flowed

all'orlo **del** **prato.**
at the edge · of the · meadow

Quand'ebbe **finito** **di** **scrivere** **si** **voltò** **a**
When (he) had · finished · -of- · to write · himself · turned · to

guardare **da** **tutte** **le** **parti,** **tanto** **era** **contento**
watch · of · all · the · parts · so much · (he) was · happy

di **trovarsi** **in** **un** **luogo** **così** **delizioso!**
of · to find himself · in · a · place · so · delicious

Quand'ecco **che** **vide** **sull'erba** **un** **Carpione** **color**
When see · that · (he) saw · on the grass · a · carp · color

dell'oro, **che** **boccheggiava** **e** **non** **ne** **poteva**
of the gold · that · gasped · and · not · itself · could

più, **perché,** **per** **la** **gola** **di** **chiappare** **dei**
(any)more · because · by · the · throat · of · to escape · of the

moscerini, aveva fatto un salto così lungo e così
gnats (he) had made a jump so long and so

fuor dell'acqua, che era andato a ricascare
our of the water that (he) was gone to fall back

sull'erba, dove stava quasi per morire.
on the grass where (he) was almost for to die

Avvenente n'ebbe compassione, e sebbene fosse
Comely of it had compassion and although (it) was
took pity on it

giorno di magro e potesse fargli comodo per
day of meager and (he) could make him comfortable for
(hunger)

il suo desinare, lo prese e lo rimesse
the his dinner him (he) took and him put back

perbenino nella corrente del fiume.
for goodness in the stream of the river

Appena il nostro Carpione sentì il fresco
Hardly -the- our carp felt the freshness

dell'acqua, cominciò a scodinzolare dall'allegrezza
of the water (it) started to wag its tail of the happiness

e andò subito a fondo: ma poi, ritornato a
and went immediately to (the) bottom but after returned at

fior d'acqua, disse, avvicinandosi tutto
(the) surface of (the) water (he) said approaching -himself- all

vispo alla riva:
lively to the shore

"Avvenente, io vi ringrazio del servizio che mi
Comely I you thank of the service that me
(for the)

avete reso; senza di voi sarei morto e voi
(you) have given without of you (I) would be dead and you

mi avete salvato. Io non sono un ingrato e
me have saved I not am an ungrateful (one) and

saprò ricambiarvi!".
(I) will know (how) to repay you

Dopo questo complimento sparì sott'acqua:
After this compliment (he) disappeared under water

e Avvenente rimase molto maravigliato dello
and Comely remained very surprised of the

spirito e della buona creanza del Carpione.
spirit and of the good nature of the carp

Un altro giorno, mentre seguitava il suo
An other day while (he) continued -the- his

viaggio, s'imbatté in un Corvo ridotto a mal
journey himself ran into in a crow reduced to (a) bad

partito: questo povero uccello era inseguito da
part this poor bird was pursued by

un'Aquila smisurata, gran divoratrice di Corvi; e
an eagle huge great devourer of crows and

stava lì lì per essere agguantato, e l'Aquila
(he) was there there for to be grabbed and the eagle

l'avrebbe inghiottito come un chicco di canapa,
it would have swallowed like a seed of hemp

se Avvenente non si fosse mosso a
if Comely not himself was moved to

compassione della povera bestia.
compassion of the poor beast

"Ecco", gli disse, "che al solito i più forti
Here him (he) said that at the usual the most strong

opprimono i più deboli. Che ragione ha l'Aquila
oppress the more weak What reason has the eagle

di mangiare il Corvo?"
of to eat the crow

E preso l'arco che portava sempre seco, e
And (he) took the bow that (he) carried always with him and

una freccia, puntò la mira contro l'Aquila e crac!
one arrow aimed the view towards the eagle and crash

le scagliò la freccia nel corpo e la passò da
him launched the arrow in the body and it passed from

parte a parte.
side to side

L'Aquila cadde giù morta, e il Corvo,
The eagle fell already dead and the crow

tutt'allegro, andandosi a posare in cima a un
all happy going himself to sit on top at a
(of)

ramo:
branch

"Avvenente", gli disse, "voi siete stato molto
Comely   him   (he) said you   are   been   very
                                     (have)

generoso d'essere venuto in aiuto a me, che sono
generous of to be come   in help to me that are
                                              (who) (is)

un povero uccello: ma non avete trovato un
a   poor   bird   but not (you) have found   an

   ingrato;   all'occorrenza   saprò
ungrateful (one)   at the occurrence   (I) will know

ricambiarvi!".
(how) to pay you back

Avvenente ammirò il buon cuore del Corvo, e
Comely   admired the good heart of the crow   and

continuò la sua strada. Una mattina, che
continued -the- his road   One   morning   that

albeggiava appena e non vedeva nemmeno dove
dawned   just   and not (he) saw   even   where

mettesse i piedi, nel traversare un gran bosco,
(he) put the feet in the to traverse a large forest

sentì un Gufo che strillava come un disperato.
(he) heard an owl that screeched like a desperate (one)

"Ohe!", egli disse, "ecco un Gufo al quale deve
Oh hey he said see an owl to -the- which must

essere capitato qualche brutto malanno."
be happened something nasty mishap
(have)

Guarda di qui, guarda di là, finalmente gli
(He) watched -of- here watched -of- there finally him

venne fatto di vedere alcune reti, che erano state
came done of to see some nets that were been

tese la notte per acchiappare gli uccelli.
stretched out the night for to catch the birds

"Che miseria!", egli disse, "si vede proprio che
What misery he said oneself sees oneself that

gli uomini sono fatti apposta per tormentarsi
the men are made expressly for to torment themselves

gli uni cogli altri, e per non lasciar ben avere
the one with the other and for not to let well have

tanti poveri animali, che non hanno fatto loro
so many poor animals that not have done them

nessun male e nessun dispetto."
no harm and no spite

Cavò fuori il suo coltello e tagliò le funicelle
(He) dug out -the- his knife and cut the cords

delle reti. Il Gufo prese il volo, ma ricalando
of the nets The owl took -the- flight but lowering

subito a tiro di schioppo:
immediately at throw of stone

"Avvenente", egli disse, "non ho bisogno di
Comely he said not (I) have need of

perdermi in parole per dirvi la gratitudine
to lose myself in words for to tell you the gratitude

che sento per voi. Il fatto parla da sé. I
that (I) feel for you The fact speaks for itself The

cacciatori stavano lì per arrivare: senza il
hunters were there for to arrive without -the-

vostro soccorso, mi avrebbero preso e
your help me (they) would have taken and

ammazzato. Ma io ho un cuore riconoscente, e
killed But I have a heart grateful and

saprò ricambiarvi".
(I) will know to repay you

Ecco le tre avventure più strepitose che
See the three adventures most amazing that

accadessero al buon Avvenente durante il
happened to -the- good Comely during -the-

suo viaggio.
his trip

Egli aveva tanta passione di arrivar presto, che,
He had so much passion of to arrive quickly that

appena giunto, andò subito al palazzo della
hardly arrived (he) went immediately to the palace of the

Bella   dai   capelli   d'oro.
Beauty of the hairs of gold

Il   palazzo   era   pieno   di   meraviglie.   Diamanti
The   palace   was   full   of   wonders   Diamonds

ammontati come sassi: abiti magnifici, argenterie,
mounted   as   stones dresses magnificent   silverware

confetti, dolci e ogni grazia di Dio: di modo che
confetti   sweets and each   grace   of God of manner that

Avvenente pensava dentro di   sé   che se la
Comely   thought   inside of himself that if the

Principessa   si   fosse decisa a lasciare tutte
princess   herself was decided to leave   all

quelle magnificenze per venire a stare col Re
those magnificences for to come to be with the king

suo padrone,   bisognava   proprio dire che gli
his master   (it) was necessary   right to say that him

era toccata una gran fortuna.
was touched a great fortune

Si   messe   un vestito di broccato e   delle
Herself (she) put on a   dress   of brocade   and of -the-

penne   bianche   e   carnicine: si   pettinò,
feathers white   and flesh colored hersef (she) combed

s'incipriò,   si   lavò   il   viso: si   infilò
herself powdered herself washed the   face   herself slipped

intorno   al   collo   una   ricca   sciarpa,   tutta
around   -at- the neck   a   rich   scarf   all

ricamata,   con un piccolo paniere e   con dentro
embroidered with a   small   basket   and with inside

un bel canino, che esso aveva comprato, passando
a   nice little dog that she   had   bought   passing

da Bologna.
by   Bologne

Avvenente era così   bello   della persona   e   così
Comely   was so   handsome of the person   and so

grazioso,   e   ogni cosa che faceva, lo   faceva con
gracious   and each thing that (he) did it   (he) did with

tanto garbo, che quando si presentò alla
so much grace that when himself (he) presented at the

porta del palazzo, tutte le guardie gli
gate of the palace all the guards (for) him

strisciarono una gran riverenza, e corsero ad
scraped a great reverence and ran to
(groveled with)

annunziare alla Bella dai capelli d'oro, che
announce to the Beauty of the hairs of gold that

Avvenente, l'ambasciatore del Re suo vicino,
Comely the ambassador of the king her neighbor

domandava la grazia di poterla vedere.
asked the grace of to be able her to see

Subito che intese il nome d'Avvenente,
Immediately that (she) understood the name of Comely

la Principessa disse: "Questo nome m'è di buon
the princess said This name me is of (a) good

augurio: scommetto che dev'essere un giovane
omen (I) wager that (it) must be a young man

grazioso e da piacere".
gracious and of to please

"Oh davvero, Signora!", dissero tutte le dame
Oh indeed Madam said all the ladies

d'onore. "Noi l'abbiamo veduto dall'ultimo piano,
of honor We him have seen from the top floor

dove s'era a mettere in ordine la vostra
where one was to put in order the your
(we were)

biancheria: e tutto il tempo che s'è
whiteness and all the time that himself (he) is
(linen)

trattenuto sotto le nostre finestre, non siamo
stayed under -the- our windows not (we) were

state più buone a far nulla."
-been- (any)more good to do nothing

"Vi fa un bell'onore", replicò la Bella dai
You make a fine honor answered the Beauty of the

capelli d'oro, "di passare il vostro tempo a
hairs of gold of to pass -the- your time to

guardare i giovanotti. Animo, via! mi si porti
watch the young men Spirit go me yourself carry
(Come on)

subito il mio vestito di gala, di raso blu, a
immediately -the- my dress of gala of satin blue at
(with)

ricami; mi si sparpaglino con grazia i
embroiderings me themselves scatted with grace -the-

miei capelli biondi: mi si faccia una ghirlanda di
my hairs blond me itself make a garland of

fiori freschi, si tirino fuori le mie scarpine
flowers fresh themselves take out the my shoes

col tacco rilevato e il mio ventaglio; si
with heel high and -the- my fan itself

spazzi la mia camera e si spolveri il mio
sweep -the- my room and itself dust -the- my

trono; perché io voglio che si dica dappertutto
throne because I want that itself says everywhere

che io sono davvero la Bella dai capelli d'oro."
that I am truly the Beauty of the hairs of gold

Ecco **tutte** **le** **donne** **in** **gran** **moto** **per**
See all the women in great motion for
(And so were)

abbigliarla **come** **una** **Regina:** **e** **tanto** **si**
to dress her like a queen and so much themselves

danno **da** **fare,** **che** **s'urtano** **fra** **di**
gave of to do that themselves bumped between of

loro **e** **non** **concludono** **nulla** **di** **buono.**
themselves and not concluded nothing of good

Finalmente **la** **Principessa** **passò** **nella** **sala** **dei**
Finally the princess passed in the hall of the

grandi **specchi** **per** **rimirarsi** **e** **vedere** **se**
great mirrors for to look at herself and to see whether

al **suo** **abbigliamento** **mancasse** **qualche** **cosa;**
to -the- her dress lacked any thing

poi **salì** **sul** **trono,** **tutto** **d'oro,** **d'avorio**
then (she) ascended on the throne all of gold of ivory

e **d'ebano,** **che** **mandava** **un** **profumo** **delizioso,** **e**
and of ebony that sent (out) a perfume delicious and

ordinò alle donne di prendere degli strumenti e
ordered to the women of to take of the instruments and

di mettersi a cantare, ma con una certa
of to set themselves to sing but with a certain

discrezione, per non cavar di cervello la gente.
discretion for not to extract of brain the people

Quando Avvenente fu condotto nella sala di
When Comely was led into the hall of

udienza, restò così fuori di sé dalla
audience (he) remained so outside of himself from the

meraviglia, che dopo ha raccontato molte
wonder that afterwards (he) has told many

volte che non poteva quasi aprir bocca per
times that not (he) could almost open (the) mouth for

parlare. Nondimeno si fece coraggio: disse il
to speak Not-of-less himself made courage said -the-
(Nonetheless) he gathered

suo discorso come non si poteva dir meglio,
his speech like not oneself could tell (it) better

e pregò la Principessa di non dargli il
and asked the Princess of not to give him the

dispiacere di doversene tornar via senza di
displeasure of to have himself of it to return -way- without -of-
(to have)

lei.
her

"Garbato Avvenente", disse la Principessa, "le
Gentle Avvenente said the Princess the

ragioni che mi avete dette sono eccellenti e io
reasons that me you have said are excellent and I

sarei contenta di fare un favore a voi, piuttosto
shall be happy of to do a favor to you rather

che a qualunqu'altra persona, Ma bisogna che
than to any other person But (it's) necessary that

sappiate che un mese fa andai a passeggiare
you know that a month ago (I) went to stroll

colle mie dame di compagnia lungo il fiume, e
with the my ladies of escort along the river and

siccome mi fu servita la colazione, così nel
since me was served the breakfast like so in the

cavarmi il guanto, mi uscì l'anello dal
taking off myself the glove me went off the ring from the

dito e disgraziatamente cadde nell'acqua.
finger and unfortunately fell in the water

Quest'anello mi è più caro del regno. Lascio
This ring me is most dear of the kingdom Let

immaginare a voi il dispiacere che provai!
immagine to you the displeasure that (I) experienced

E ora ho fatto giuro di non dare ascolto a
And now (I) have made (an) oath of not to give hearing to

nessuna trattativa di matrimonio, se l'ambasciatore
none deal of matrimony if the ambassador
(any) marriage deal

che verrà a portarmi lo sposo non mi riporti
that will come to take me the spouse not me brings

prima il mio anello. Tocca a voi a decidere su
first -the- my ring Touches to you to decide on
(It is)

quello che volete fare; perché se duraste a
that what (you) want to do because if (you) endure to

parlarmene quindici giorni e quindici notti in
talk to me of it fifteen days and fifteen nights in

fila, non arrivereste mai a farmi cambiare di
(a) row not (you) will arrive ever at to make me change of

sentimento."
sentiment
(opinion)

Avvenente rimase mezzo intontito a questa
Comely remained half surprised at this

risposta: le fece una gran riverenza e la
answer her (he) made a great reverence and her
(bow)

pregò di voler gradire il canino, il paniere e
asked of to want appreciate the little dog the basket and
(to accept)

la sciarpa; ma essa rispose che non accettava
the scarf but that one answered that not (she) accepted
(she)

nessun regalo e che pensasse alle cose che
no gift and that (she) thought at the things that
(she would think) (of the)

gli aveva dette.
he had said

Quando fu tornato a casa, se ne andò a
When was returned to house himself of it went to
(he had)

letto senza prendere nemmeno un boccone da
bed without to take -not- even a mouthful of

cena: e il canino, che si chiamava Caprioletto,
dinner and the little dog that itself called Caprioletto

non volle cenare neanche lui e andò a
not wanted to dine neither him and went to

coricarsi accanto al padrone.
go to bed himself next to the master

Tutta la notte, quanto fu lunga, Avvenente non
All the night which was long Comely not

fece altro che sospirare. "Dove poss'io
did other than sigh Where can I
(anything else)

ripescare un anello, che, un mese fa, è cascato
fish up a ring that a month ago is fallen

nel fiume?", esso diceva. "Sarebbe una pazzia
in the river that one said (It) would be a foolishness
(he)

soltanto a provarsi! Si vede bene che la
even to try itself Oneself sees well that the

Principessa lo ha detto apposta per mettermi
Princess it has said precisely for to put me

nell'impossibilità di poterla ubbidire."
in the impossibility of to be able her to obey

E tornava a sospirare e a dare in tutte le
And turned to sigh and to give in all the
(he started again)

smanie. Caprioletto, che lo sentiva, gli disse:
agitations Caprioletto that him heard him said

"Caro padrone, fatemi un piacere: non disperate
Dear master do me a pleasure not despair yourself
(favor)

ancora della vostra buona fortuna. Voi siete un
yet of the your good fortune You are a

giovine troppo carino, per non dover essere
youth too dear for not to have to be

fortunato. Appena farà giorno, andiamo
fortunate Hardly (it) will make day (we will) go
(lucky) (it will be)

subito in riva al fiume".
immediately in (the) bank to the river
(to) (of the)

Avvenente gli dette colla mano due buffetti e
Comely him gave with the hand two cuffs and

non rispose sillaba: finché stanco e rifinito dalla
not answered (a) syllable until tired out and finished by the

passione, si addormentò.
emotion himself fell asleep

Caprioletto, quando vide i primi chiarori
Caprioletto when (he) saw the first clearings

dell'alba, cominciò tanto a sgambettare, che lo
of the dawn started so much to move about that him

svegliò e gli disse: "Animo, padrone, vestitevi:
(he) awoke and him said Spirit master dress yourself

e usciamo!".
and let's go out

Avvenente non desiderava di meglio. Si alza,
Comely not desired of better Himself rose

si veste, scende nel giardino e dal
himself dressed descended into the garden and from the

giardino s'incammina un passo dietro l'altro
garden himself walked a pace behind the other

verso il fiume, dove si mette a passeggiare
towards the river where himself (he) set to stroll
(he began)

col suo cappello sugli occhi e colle braccia
with his hat on the eyes and with the arms

incrociate, pensando al brutto momento di
crossed thinking at the nasty moment of

dover ripartire, quand'ecco che a un tratto
to have to leave again when here that at a stretch

sente una voce che lo chiama: "Avvenente!
(he) heard a voice that him called Comely

Avvenente!".
Comely

Si   volta a guardare da tutte le parti e non
Himself turned to look of all the parts and not
everywhere

vede anima viva. Credé di aver sognato. Si
sees soul alive (He) thought of to have dreamed Himself

rimette a passeggiare, e daccapo la solita voce
set again to stroll and from-head the usual voice
(again)

a chiamarlo: "Avvenente! Avvenente!".
to call him Comely Comely

"Chi è che mi chiama?", diss'egli.
Who and who me calls said he

Caprioletto, che era molto piccino, e così
Caprioletto that was very small and as such

poteva guardare nell'acqua a piccolissima distanza,
could look in the water at very little distance

gli rispose: "Datemi del bugiardo se non è un
him answered Give me of the liar if not (it) is a

Carpione, color dell'oro, quello laggiù in fondo".
Carp color of the gold that there down in bottom

Detto fatto, un grosso Carpio venne su a
Said (and) done a large Carp came up to

fior d'acqua e gli disse:
(the) surface of (the) water and him said

"Voi mi avete salvato la vita nei prati degli
You me had saved the life in the praries of the

Alzieri, dove io senza di voi sarei rimasto morto,
Alzieri where I without of you would be remained dead

e vi promisi un ricambio. Pigliate, caro
and you (I) promised an exchange Catch yourself dear
                                 (returned favor)

Avvenente, ecco qui l'anello della Bella dai capelli
Comely here here the ring of the Beauty of the hairs
         (see)

d'oro".
of gold

Egli si chinò e tirò fuori l'anello dalla
He himself bowed (down) and pulled out the ring of the

gola del Carpio e lo ringraziò a mille doppi.
throat of the Carp and him thanked to thousand double
                                        a thousand times

E invece di tornare a casa, andò difilato al
And instead of to return to house (he) went straight to the

palazzo, in compagnia di Caprioletto, che era
palace in company of Caprioletto that was
(who)

contento come una pasqua per aver consigliato
happy like an Easter for to have advised

il suo padrone a venire sulla sponda del
-the- his master to come to the side of the

fiume.
river

Fu annunziato alla Principessa che Avvenente
(It) was announced to the Princess that Comely

desiderava di vederla.
desired of to see her

"Ahimè! povero giovane!", diss'ella, "e' vien da me
Oh my poor youth said she (he) is come to me

per congedarsi. Avrà capito che ciò
for to take leave of himself (He) will have understood that it

che io voglio da lui è impossibile, e partirà
that I want from him is impossible and (he) will leave

per andare a raccontarlo al suo padrone."
for to go to tell it to -the- his master

Avvenente, appena introdotto, le presentò l'anello
Comely hardly introduced her presented the ring
(as soon as)

dicendo: "Ecco, o Principessa, il vostro
saying Here oh Princess -the- your

comando è stato obbedito: sareste ora tanto
command is been obeyed will (you) be now so
(has)

compiacente di prendere per vostro sposo il
complacent of to take as your spouse -the-
(nice)

mio augusto padrone?".
my august patron

Quand'ella vide il suo anello, sano e salvo
When she saw -the- her ring sane and safe

come se non fosse stato toccato, rimase
like if not was been touched (she) remained
(it had)

meravigliata: ma tanto meravigliata, che credeva
surprised / but / so / surprised / that / (she) believed

di sognare.
of / to dream

"Davvero", ella disse, "grazioso Avvenente! Si vede
Really / she / said / thanks / Comely / One / sees

proprio che voi avete una fata dalla vostra
truly / that / you / have / a / fairy / of the / yours

altrimenti questi miracoli non si fanno."
otherwise / these / miracles / not / themselves / make (happen)

"Signora", egli replicò, "io non so di fate: ma
Lady / he / replied / I / not / know / of / fairies / but

so che ho un gran desiderio di contentare
(I) know / that / (I) have / a / great / desire / of / to fulfill

ogni vostra voglia."
each / your / want

"Poiché avete questa buona volontà", ella
Then / (you) have / this / good / will / she

continuò "rendetemi un altro gran servizio, senza
continued render you me an other great service without

di che non c'è caso che io possa risolvermi
of that not there is case that I can decide myself
(possibility)

a prendere marito. C'è un Principe, non
to take (a) husband There is a Prince not

lontano di qui, detto Galifrone, il quale si
far from here said Galifrone the which himself
(a certain)

è messo in testa di volermi sposare. Egli mi ha
is put in head of to want me to marry He me has

fatto conoscere la sua intenzione con minacce
made to know -the- his intention with threats

paurose, dicendo che se io non lo voglio, metterà
fearful saying that if I not it want (he) will put

lo scompiglio e la desolazione ne' miei Stati.
the chaos and the desolation in the my Estates
(country)

Ma ditemi un po' voi, se potrei dargli retta.
But tell me a bit you if (I) can give him right
(correction)

Figuratevi che è un gigante più grande di
Figure yourself that (he) is a giant more large of
(than)

una gran torre; ed è capace di mangiare un
a large tower and (he) is capable of to eat a

uomo come una scimmia mangerebbe una
man like a monkey would eat a

castagna. Quando va in giro per la
chestnut When (he) goes in round by the

campagna, si mette in tasca dei piccoli
countryside himself puts in (the) pocket of the small

cannoni, dei quali poi si serve come se
cannons of the which then himself (he) serves as if

fossero pistole: e quando parla forte,
(they) were pistols and when (he) speaks loud

fa diventar sorde tutte le persone che gli
(he) makes become deaf all the persons that him

stanno vicine. Gli mandai a dire che non avevo
stand close Him (I) ordered to say that not (I) have

voglia di maritarmi e che mi scusasse: ma non
want of to marry myself and that me (I) excuse but not

per questo ha smesso di perseguitarmi: ammazza
for this has stopped of to persecute me (I) kills

i miei sudditi, e prima d'ogni cosa bisogna
the my subjects and first of every thing necessary
(of any)

che voi vi battiate con lui, e che mi
(is) that you yourself battle with him and that me

portiate la sua testa."
(you) carry -the- his head

Avvenente rimase sbalordito da questo discorso:
Comely remained aghast of this discourse

stette un po' soprappensiero; poi disse: "Ebbene,
(he) stood a bit under-thought then (he) said (It) is well
(thinking)

o signora! io mi batterò con Galifrone. Credo
oh lady I myself will battle with Galifrone (I) believe

che ne toccherò io! A ogni modo, morirò da
that of it will touch I At each manner (I) will die of
(any)

valoroso".
valorous

La Principessa restò meravigliatissima: e gli
The Princess remained very surprised and him

disse un monte di cose, per vedere di
said a mount of things for to see of

stornarlo da questa impresa. Ma non
to turn away him from this enterprise But not

valse a nulla. Egli se ne venne via, per
(it) mattered to nothing He himself of it came away for

mettersi subito in cerca delle armi e di
to set himself immediately in search of the arms and of

tutto l'occorrente.
all the necessary

Quand'ebbe ciò che voleva, ripose Caprioletto
When (he) had that what (he) wanted packed away Caprioletto

nel solito panierino, montò sul suo bel
in the usual little basket climbed on the his beautiful

cavallo e andò nel paese di Galifrone. A
horse and went into the land of Galifrone To

quanti incontrava per via, domandava a tutti
those (he) encountered on (the) road (he) asked to all

notizie di lui: e tutti gli dicevano che era un
notices of him and all him said that (he) was a

vero demonio, e che faceva spavento soltanto a
true demon and that (it) did fear just by

doverlo avvicinare. Caprioletto, per fargli
to have to him approach Caprioletto for to make him

coraggio, gli diceva: "Caro padrone, in quel mentre
courage him said Dear master in that while

che vi batterete, io anderò a mordergli le
that yourself (you) will battle I will go to bite him the

gambe: lui si chinerà per levarmi di tra
legs he himself will bow down for to take me from behind

i piedi, e intanto voi l'ammazzerete".
the feet and meanwhile you him will kill

Avvenente ammirava lo spirito del suo canino:
Comely admired the spirit of -the- his little dog

ma sapeva bene che il suo aiuto non sarebbe
but (he) knew well that -the- his help not would be

stato in ragione del bisogno.
been in reason of the need
(proportion)

Finalmente arrivò in vicinanza del castello di
Finally arrived in (the) neighborhood of the castle of

Galifrone: tutte le strade erano seminate d'ossa
Galifrone all the streets were sown of bone

e di carcasse d'uomini, che esso aveva divorati
and of carcasses of men that this one had devoured
(he)

o fatti in pezzi. Né dové aspettarlo molto
or made in pieces Neither (he) had to await him (a) lot
(ripped)

tempo, perché lo vide comparire di dietro
(of) time because him (he) saw appear from behind

al bosco. La sua testa sorpassava gli alberi
to the wood -The- his head surpassed the trees

più   alti,   e   con   una   voce   spaventosa   cantava:
more high and with   a   voice   fearful   sung

Chi   mi   porta   dei   teneri   bambini
That me (you) carry of the tender   children

Da   farli   scricchiolare sotto   il   dente?
Of to make them   crunch   under the   teeth

Ne   ho   bisogno di tanti   e   poi di tanti.
Of it (I) have   need   of many and then of many

Che in tutto il mondo non ce   n'è   bastanti.
That in   all   the world   not there of it is   enough

E   subito   Avvenente,   a   botta   e   risposta,
And immediately Comely   at shock and   reply

   si   messe a cantare:
himself   set   to   sing

Fatti avanti,   c'è   Avvenente
Done before there is   Comely

Che saprà strapparti   i   denti;
That will know to tear out the   teeth

Non è un colosso di figura,
Not (it) is a colossus of figure

Ma di te non ha paura.
But of you not (he) has fear

Le rime non tornavano precise: ma bisogna
The rhymes not turned precise but necessary

riflettere che la strofa la improvvisò in fretta e
to reflect that the sentence it improvised in haste and

in furia, ed è un miracolo se non la fece
in fury and (it) is a miracle if not it (he) made

anche più brutta, per la paura che gli era
also more ugly for the fear that him was

entrata in corpo. Quando Galifrone sentì questa
entered in body When Galifrone felt this

risposta, si voltò di qua e di là, e vide
response himself turned of there and of there and saw

Avvenente colla spada nel pugno della mano,
Comely with the sword in the fist of the hand

che gli disse per giunta tre o quattro parolacce,
that him said for together three or four bad words

per farlo andare in bestia più che mai. Non
for to make him go in beast more that ever Not
(than)

ci mancava altro!
itself lacked other

Egli prese una furia così spaventosa, che, afferrata
He took a fury so fearful that gripped

una mazza tutta di ferro, avrebbe ucciso con un
a mace all of iron had killed with one

colpo solo il delicato Avvenente, senza il caso
strike only the delicate Comely without the case

di un Corvo che venne a posarglisi sulla testa e
of a Crow that came to set him itself on the head and

gli dette negli occhi una beccata così aggiustata,
him said in the eyes a beak so fixed

che glieli cavò di netto.
that of him them dug out -of- clean

Il sangue gli grondava giù per il viso: e
The blood him dripped down by the face and

infuriato da far paura, picchiava mazzate a
furious of to make fear (he) beat heavy blows to

diritto e a rovescio. Intanto Avvenente,
ahead and to (the) back Meanwhile Comely

scansandosi a tempo, gli tirava dei colpi di
dodging himself at time him pulled from the blows of
(in)

spada, ficcandogliela in corpo fino
sword thrusting him there in (the) body up

all'impugnatura: e tanto era il sangue, che il
to the hilt and so much was the blood that the

gigante perdeva dalle sue molte ferite, che
giant lost from the his many wounds that

finalmente stramazzò per terra.
finally (he) fell heavily on (the) ground

Avvenente gli tagliò subito la testa, tutto
Comely him cut (off) immediately the head all

allegro di avere avuto questa bella fortuna; e
happy of to have had this beautiful fortune and
(good)

il Corvo che s'era posato sul ramo d'un
the Crow that himself was set on the branch of a
(himself had)

albero, gli disse:
tree him said

"Io non ho dimenticato il servizio che mi
I not have forgotten the service that me

rendeste, uccidendo l'Aquila che mi dava addosso.
(you) rendered killing the Eagle that me gave on-back
assaulted

Vi promisi di contraccambiarvi, e credo di
You (I) promised of to reward you in return and (I) believe of

aver pagato il mio debito".
to have paid -the- my debt

"Sono io che vi debbo tutto, signor Corvo",
Am I that you owe everything Mr. Crow
(It is)

rispose Avvenente, "e mi dichiaro vostro buon
answered Comely and myself (I) declare your good

servitore."
servant

Poi montò subito a cavallo, col carico
Then (he) mounted immediately at horse with the load

della spaventosa testa di Galifrone.
of the frightful head of Galifrona

Quando arrivò in città, tutta la gente gli
When (he) arrived in (the) city all the people him

andava dietro gridando: "Ecco il bravo Avvenente,
went after shouting Here the brave Comely
(See)

che ritorna dall'aver morto il gigante Galifrone"
that returns of the to have killed the giant Galifrone
(of having)

e la Principessa, che sentiva questo baccano e
and the Princess that heard this racket and

tremava dalla paura che venissero a dargli la
trembled of the fear that (they) came to give her the

nuova della morte di Avvenente, non aveva fiato di
news of the death of Comely not had faith of

chiedere che cosa fosse avvenuto. Ma in quel
to believe what thing was become But in that
had happened

punto ella vide entrare Avvenente, colla testa
point she saw enter Comely with the head
(moment)

del gigante, che metteva ancora spavento,
of the giant that set still fear

quantunque non potesse più fare alcun male.
although not could (any)more do any harm

"Signora", egli disse, "il vostro nemico è morto.
Lady he said -the- your enemy is dead

Voglio sperare che ora non direte più di no
(I) want to expect that now not (you) say (any)more -of- no

al Re, mio augusto padrone."
to -the- King my august master

"Ah! senza dubbio", replicò la Bella dai capelli
Ah without doubt answered the Beauty of the hairs

d'oro, "che io gli dirò sempre di no, se voi
of gold that I him will say always of no if you

prima della mia partenza non trovate il modo di
first of the my leaving not find the manner of
(before)

portarmi l'acqua della caverna tenebrosa. C'è
to carry me the water of the cavern dark There is

qui, poco distante, una grotta profonda che gira
here little distant a cave deep that turns
(runs)

più di cento chilometri. Ci stanno
more of (a) hundred kilometers There stand
(than)

sull'ingresso due draghi che ne impediscono
on the threshold two dragons that of it forbid

l'entrata. Buttano fiamme di fuoco dalla bocca
the entrance (They) throw flames of fire from the mouth

e dagli occhi. Quando poi siamo dentro alla
and from the eyes When then (we) are inside -to- the

grotta, si trova una gran buca nella quale
cave oneself finds a great opening in the which

bisogna scendere, ed è piena di rospi, di
(it is) necessary to descend and it) is filled of toads of

biacchi, di ramarri e di altri serpenti. In fondo
rat snakes of lizards and of other snakes In bottom
(On the)

a questa buca c'è una piccola nicchia, dalla
to this pit there is a small niche of the

quale scaturisce la fontana della bellezza e
which springs the fountain of -the- beauty and

della salute: io voglio a tutti i costi di
of -the- health I want at all the costs of

quell'acqua. Ogni cosa che si lava con
that water Every thing that itself washes with

quell'acqua diventa meravigliosa: se siamo belle,
that water becomes wonderful if (we) are beautiful

si rimane sempre belle: se brutte, si diventa
one remains always beautiful if ugly one becomes

belle: se siamo giovani, si resta giovani: se
beautiful if (we) are young we remain young if

vecchie, si ringiovanisce. Vedete bene, caro
old one rejuvenates (You) see well dear

Avvenente, che io non posso lasciare il mio
Comely   that I not can   let -the- my

Regno, senza portar meco un poco di quell'acqua
Reign without to carry me-with a bit of that water
(with me)

lì."
there

"Signora", egli rispose; "voi siete tanto bella, che
Lady   he answered you are so beautiful that

quest'acqua per voi mi pare affatto inutile: ma io
this water for you me seems in fact useless but I

sono un ambasciatore disgraziato, di cui volete
am an ambassador disgraced of who (you) want

la morte. Io vado a cercarvi ciò che voi
the death I go to search (for) you that what you

desiderate, colla certezza nel cuore di non
desire with the certainty in the heart of not

tornare più indietro."
to return (any)more back

La Bella dai capelli d'oro non cambiò per questo
The Beauty of the hairs of gold not changed for this

di proposito: e il povero Avvenente partì
of intention and the poor Comely left

col suo canino Caprioletto per andare alla
with -the- his little dog Caprioletto for to go to the

grotta tenebrosa, a cercarvi l'acqua della
cave dark to search there the water of the

bellezza.
beauty

Tutti quelli che lo incontravano lungo la strada,
All those that him encountered along the road

dicevano: "Che peccato vedere un giovane tanto
said What sin to see a youth so
(shame)

grazioso correre così spensieratamente in bocca
gracious run so thoughtlessly in mouth

alla morte: egli se ne va alla grotta da
to the death he himself of it goes to the cave by

sé   solo: ma quand'anche fossero cento, non
himself alone but when also (there) were (a) hundred not

verrebbero a capo di nulla. Perché la Principessa
would come to head of nothing Because the Princess

s'incaponisce a volere l'impossibile?". Egli
herself puts in the head to want the impossible He

seguitava a camminare, e non diceva parola: ma
continued to walk and not said (a) word but

era triste, molto triste.
(he) was sad very sad

Arrivato verso la cima della montagna, si
Arrived towards the top of the mountain himself
(Arriving)

sedette per ripigliar fiato, e lasciò il cavallo a
sat for to recatch breath and let the horse to

pascere e Caprioletto a correr dietro alle
pasture and Caprioletto to run behind to the

mosche. Egli sapeva che la grotta tenebrosa non
flies He knew that the cave dark not

era molto distante di là, e guardava se per
was very far of there and looked if by

caso l'avesse potuta scoprire; quand'ecco che
case it had been able to discover when here that
(chance)

vide un enorme scoglio, nero come l'inchiostro,
(he) saw an enormous cliff black like the ink

di dove usciva un fumo densissimo, e di lì
from where exited a smoke very dense and from there

a poco uno dei draghi che buttava fuoco dagli
to little one of the dragons that threw fire from the

occhi e dalla gola. Il drago aveva il corpo
eyes and from the throat The dragon had the body

verde e giallo, dei grossi unghioni e una
green and yellow -of- the great claws and a

coda lunghissima, che s'attorcigliava in più di
tail very long that himself entwined in more of
(than)

cento giri. Caprioletto vide anch'egli ogni cosa,
(a) hundred rounds Caprioletto saw also he every thing

e   non sapeva dove nascondersi: la povera bestia
and not   knew   where to hide himself the   poor   beast

era mezza morta dalla paura.
was   half   dead of -the- fear

Avvenente, fatto oramai animo di morire, cavò
Comely   made   now   spirit of to die   dug

fuori la sua spada e   s'avviò   colla   sua
away -the- his sword and himself set out with -the- his

boccetta, che la Bella dai capelli d'oro gli aveva
small bottle that the Beauty of the   hairs of gold him   had

dato, per riempirla coll'acqua della bellezza. Egli
given   for to fill it with the water of the   beauty   He

disse   al   suo canino Caprioletto:
said   to -the- his little dog Caprioletto

"Per me è finita! io non   potrò   mai arrivare a
For   me (it) is finished I not will be able ever to arrive to
                                                          (to manage)

prendere di quest'acqua, che è custodita dai
take   of   this water   that (it) is guarded of the
                                                   (by the)

draghi; quando   sarò   morto, riempi la boccetta
dragons   when   (it) will be dead   (I) fill the little bottle

col   mio sangue e portala alla Principessa,
with -the-   my   blood   and carry it to the   Princess

perché ella possa vedere quanto mi costa il
because   she could   see   how much me (it) costs the

servirla: e   dopo vai a trovare il Re mio
to serve her and after (I) go to find   the King my
(serving her)

padrone, e raccontagli la mia disgrazia".
master   and   tell him   the my   disgrace

Mentre   diceva così,   sentì   una voce che lo
Meanwhile   (he) said such (he) heard   a   voice that him

chiamava: "Avvenente! Avvenente!".
called   Comely   Comely

Egli disse: "Chi mi chiama?", e vide un Gufo nel
He   said Who me   calls   and saw a   Owl in the

buco d'un albero vecchio, che gli disse: "Voi mi
hole   of a   tree   old   that him said You me

avete liberato dalle reti de' cacciatori, dov'ero
had freed of the nets of the hunters where (I) was

rimasto preso: e mi salvaste la vita. Promisi di
remained caught and me (you) saved the life (I) promise of

rendervi il contraccambio, e il momento è
to render you the counter-exchange and the moment is
(reward)

giunto. Datemi la vostra boccetta: io conosco tutti
arrived Give me the your little bottle I know all

gli andirivieni della grotta tenebrosa: anderò io
the goings and comings of the cave dark will go I

a prendervi l'acqua della bellezza".
to to take you the water of the beauty

Figuratevi se questa cosa gli fece piacere! Lo
Figure yourself if this thing him made please It

lascio pensare a voi. Avvenente gli dette
(I) let to think -to- you Comely him gave
(to imagine)

subito la sua boccetta e il Gufo entrò
immediately -the- his bottle and the Owl entered

nella grotta, come sarebbe entrato in casa sua.
in the   cave   like   (it) would be   entered   in   house   his

E in meno d'un quarto d'ora tornò e
And   in   less   of a   quarter   of hour   turned   and
           (than a)   (than an hour) (returned)

riportò la boccetta piena e tappata.
brought back   the   bottle   full   and   corked

Ad Avvenente parve d'aver toccato il cielo
To   Comely   (it) seemed   of to have   touched   the   sky

con un dito: ringraziò il Gufo dal profondo
with   a   finger   (I) thanked   the   Owl   from the   depth

del cuore e, risalita la montagna, prese
of the   heart   and   went back out   the   mountain   took
            (went back down from)

tutt'allegro la strada che menava alla città.
all happy   the   street   that   led   to the   city

Andò subito al palazzo e presentò la
(He) went   immediately   to the   palace   and   (he) presented   the

boccetta alla Bella dai capelli d'oro, la quale
little bottle   to the   Beauty   of the   hairs   of gold   the   which

non ebbe più nulla da ridire.
not had (any)more nothing of to find fault

Ella ringraziò Avvenente, e diè l'ordine che
She thanked Comely and gave the order that

fosse allestita ogni cosa per la partenza. Poi
(she) was prepared every thing for the departure Then

si messe in viaggio con lui: e strada facendo,
herself (she) put in travel with him and street making

finì col persuadersi che il giovinetto era
until with the to persuade himself that the youth was

molto grazioso; e qualche volta gli diceva: "Se
very grateful and (at) some time him (she) said If

aveste voluto, vi avrei fatto Re e non
(you) had wanted you would have made King and not

saremmo partiti mai dai miei Stati". Ma egli
(we) would be left ever from the my States But he
                                        (Country)

rispose: "Rinunzierei a tutti i troni della terra,
answered (I) would renounce to all the thrones of the earth

piuttosto che dare un dispiacere così forte   al
rather   that to give a   displeasure   so   strong to -the-
(than)

mio Re: sebbene voi siate più bella   del   sole".
my King even if you are more beautiful of the   sun
                                       (than the)

Finalmente giunsero alla Capitale, e il Re,
Finally   arrived   at the   Capital   and the King

sapendo che la Bella dai capelli d'oro stava per
knowing that the Beauty of the hairs of gold stood for

arrivare, andò a incontrarla e le presentò i
to arrive went to meet her and her presented the

più bei regali del mondo.
most beautiful gifts of the world

Furono fatte le nozze, e con tanta gala e
Were made the nuptials and with so much pomp and
                  (marriage)

magnificenza, che si durò a discorrerne per un
magnificence that itself lasted to talk of it for a

pezzo; ma la Bella dai capelli d'oro, che in
while but the Beauty of the hairs of gold that in

fondo   al   cuore   era   innamorata   di   Avvenente,
depth   of the heart   was   in love   of   Comely

non poteva stare senza vederlo   e   l'aveva sempre
not could   be   without to see him and him had always

sulla bocca.
on the mouth

Ella diceva   al   Re: "Se non   era   Avvenente, io
She   said to the King If not (it) was Comely   I

non sarei   dicerto   venuta qui: egli ha fatto per
not would be certainly come   here he   has made   for

me   delle   cose, da non   potersi   credere; e
me -of the- things of not to be able oneself to believe and

voi dovete essergli grato".
you   must   be him   grateful

Gl'invidiosi   che   sentivano questi discorsi della
The jealous ones that   heard   these   talks   of the

Regina andavano dopo bisbigliando   al   Re: "Voi
Queen   went   after whispering to the King You

non siete geloso; eppure avreste motivo di
not were jealous nevertheless (you) will have motive of

esserlo. La Regina è così innamorata di
to be it The Queen is so in love of
(with)

Avvenente, che non mangia né beve più;
Comely that not (she) eats nor (she) drinks (any) more

essa non fa altro che parlar di lui e della
that one not does other than to talk of him and of the
(she)

grande riconoscenza che voi dovete avergli:
great gratefulness that you must to have to him

come se chiunque altro aveste mandato, nel
as if anyone else (you) had sent in the

posto suo, non avesse saputo fare altrettanto".
place (of) his not had known to do different

E il Re disse: "Davvero, che me ne sono
And the King said Really that me of it am

accorto anch'io. Che sia preso subito e
noticed also I That (he) is taken immediately and

imprigionato nella torre, coi ferri ai piedi e
imprisoned in the tower with the irons at the feet and

alle mani".
at the hands

Avvenente fu preso e, in ricompensa di aver
Comely was taken and in compensation of to have

così bene servito il Re, fu chiuso nella torre
so well served the King was closed in the tower

coi ferri ai piedi e alle mani. La sola
with the irons at the feet and to the hands The only

persona che egli vedesse, era il guardiano della
person that he saw was the guard of the

carcere; il quale gli gettava da una buca un
prison the which him threw of one hole a

pezzo di pan nero e un po' d'acqua in una
piece of bread black and a bit of water in a

ciotola di terra. Ma il suo piccolo Caprioletto
bowl of earth But -the- his little Caprioletto

non lo abbandonava mai, e veniva a fargli
not him abandoned ever and came to make him
(give him)

coraggio e a portargli tutte le nuove che
courage and to carry him all the news that

correvano per la città.
ran through the city

Quando la Bella dai capelli d'oro venne a
When the Beauty of the hairs of gold came to

risapere la disgrazia di Avvenente, andò a
know of the disgrace of Comely went to

buttarsi ai piedi del Re, e colle lacrime
throw himself to the feet of the King and with the tears

agli occhi lo pregò a farlo levare di prigione.
at the eyes him asked to make him take (out) of prison

Ma più essa si raccomandava, e più
But (the) more she herself urged and (the) more

il Re s'intristiva, pensando fra sé e
the King himself saddened thinking between himself and

sé: "È segno che ne è innamorata" e
himself (It) is sign that with him (she) is in love and

così non intendeva né ragioni né preghiere.
like so not intended neither reasons nor prayers
(arguments)

Il Re finì col mettersi in testa di
The King finished with -the- to put himself in (the) head of

non essere abbastanza bello agli occhi della
not to be enough beautiful at the eyes of the
(in the)

Regina: e gli venne l'idea di lavarsi il viso
Queen and him came the idea of to wash himself the face

coll'acqua della bellezza, per vedere se in questo
with the water of the beauty for to see if in this

modo gli fosse riuscito di farsi amare un
manner him was succeeded of to make himself love a

poco di più. Quest'acqua stava sul caminetto
bit of more This water was on the little fireplace

nella camera della Regina, che la teneva lì, per
in the chamber of the Queen that it kept there for

averla sempre sott'occhio; ma una delle sue
to have it always under eye but one of -the- her

cameriere, volendo ammazzare un ragno con una
chambermaids wanting to kill a spider with a

spazzolata, fece cascare disgraziatamente la
brush made fall unfortunately the

boccetta, la quale si ruppe, e l'acqua se
little bottle the which itself broke and the water itself

n'andò tutta per la terra. La cameriera ripuli
of it went all on the ground The chambermaid cleaned up

ogni cosa in fretta e furia, e non sapendo
every thing in haste and fury and not knowing

come rimediarla, si ricordò di aver visto nel
how to fix it she remembered of to have seen in the

gabinetto del Re un'altra boccetta
cabinet of the King an other bottle

somigliantissima e piena d'acqua chiara, tale e
similar and filled of water clear such and

quale come l'acqua della bellezza. Non parendo
which like the water of the beauty Not (over)thinking

suo fatto, la prese senza star a dir nulla e la
her deed it took without to stay to say nothing and it

posò sul camminetto della Regina.
set on the little fireplace of the Queen

L'acqua che era nel gabinetto del Re serviva
The water that was in the cabinet of the King served

per far morire i Principi e i grandi
for to make die the Princes and the great

Signori, quando ne avevano fatta qualcuna delle
Lords when of it (they) had made some of the

grosse. Invece di tagliar loro la testa o impiccarli,
greats Instead of to cut them the head or to hang them
(mistakes)

si bagnava loro il viso con quest'acqua: e
themselves bathed them the face with this water and

così si addormentavano e non si
like so itself fell asleep and not themselves

svegliavano   più.   Una   sera,   dunque,   il   Re
awoke   (any)more   An   evening   therefore   the   King

prese   la   boccetta   e   si   strofinò   ben   bene   il
took   the   little bottle   and   himself   rubbed   well   well   the
                                                                very well

viso.   Dopo   si   addormentò   e   morì.
face   After (that)   -himself-   (he) fell asleep   and   died

Il   piccolo   Caprioletto,   che   fu   uno   dei   primi   a
The   little   Caprioletto   that   was   one   of   (the) first   to

sapere   il   caso,   andò   subito   a   raccontarlo
know   (of) the   case   went   immediately   to   tell it

ad   Avvenente,   il   quale   gli   disse   di   andare   di
to   Comely   the   which   him   said   of   to go   of
                                                                (on)

corsa   dalla   Bella   dai   capelli   d'oro   e   di   pregarla
(a) run   of the   Beauty   of the   hairs   of gold   and   of   to ask her
            (to the)

a   volersi   ricordare   del   povero   prigioniero.
to   want herself   remember   -of- the   poor   prisoner

Caprioletto   sgattaiolò   fra   mezzo   alle   gambe
Caprioletto   slipped   between   (the) middle   to the   legs
                                                                (of the)

della folla, perché alla Corte c'era un gran
of the crowd because to the Court there was a great

via-vai e una gran diceria per la
coming and going and a great rumor because of the

morte del Re, e disse alla Regina: "Signora,
death of the King and said to the Queen Lady

non vi scordate del povero Avvenente".
not you forget of the poor Comely

Ella si rammentò subito di tutti i
She herself remembered immediately of all the

patimenti che aveva sofferti per lei, e della sua
sufferings that (he) had suffered for her and of -the- his

gran fidatezza.
great trust

Uscì senza farne parola con alcuno, e
(She) exited without to make of it word with anyone and

andò diritto alla torre, dove sciolse da se
went directly to the tower where (she) unfastened by herself
(her-)

stessa le catene dalle mani e dai piedi
self   the   chains   from the   hands   and   from the   feet

d'Avvenente: e mettendogli una corona in capo
of Comely   and   putting him   a   crown   in   (the) head
                                                        (on)

e un manto reale sulle spalle, disse: "Venite,
and   a   mantle   royal   on the   shoulders   said   Come

mio caro Avvenente, io vi faccio Re, e vi
my   dear   Comely   I   you   make   King   and   you

prendo per mio sposo".
take   for   my   spouse
(as)

Egli si gettò ai suoi piedi e la ringraziò:
He   himself   threw   to -the-   her   feet   and   her   thanked

e tutti si chiamarono fortunati di averlo
and   all   themselves   called   fortunate   of   to have him

per sovrano. Le nozze furono fatte con
for   sovereign   The   nuptials   were   made   with
(as)   (wedding)   (was)

grandissima magnificenza, e la Bella dai capelli
very great   magnificence   and   the   Beauty   of the   hairs

d'oro visse molti anni col suo bell'Avvenente,
of gold / lived / many / years / with -the- / her / beautiful Comely

tutti e due felici e contenti, da non
all / and / two / happy / and / satisfied / of / not

poterselo figurare.
to be able oneself it / to imagine

Si vuole che Avvenente lasciasse ai suoi
Itself / wants / that / Comely / lets / to -the- / his

figli un libro di ricordi: un libro curioso, perché
children / a / book / of / memories / a / book / curious / because

aveva tutte le pagine bianche, meno l'ultima,
(it) had / all / the / pages / white (empty) / less (except for) / the last (one)

sulla quale aveva scritto di proprio pugno le
on the / which / (he) had / written / of (with) / (his) own / fist (hand) / the

seguenti parole:
following / words

"Se per caso qualche povero diavolo ricorre a te
If / by case (per chance) / some / poor / devil / occurs (happens) / to / you

per   essere   aiutato,   tu   aiutalo: né   badare
for   to be   helped   you   help him   neither   pay attention

com'è   vestito,   né   se   abbia   viso   di   persona   da
how (he) is   dressed   nor   if   (he) had   face   of   (a) person   of

poterti   rendere,   un   giorno   o   l'altro,   il
to be able to you   to render   one   day   or   the other   the
              (to return)

piacere   che   gli   fai.
pleasure   that   him   (you) make

Sulle   opere   buone   e   generose   non   si
On the   works   good   and   generous   not   oneself

mercanteggia   mai: né   bisogna   farle
haggles   never   neither   (you) need   to make it

coll'intenzione   di   ripigliarci   sopra   il   frutto   e
with the intention   of   to pick up us   on   the   fruit   and

l'usura.
the usury

A   ogni   modo,   tieni   sempre   a   mente   che   un
At   each   manner   keep   always   at   mind   that   a
                                            (in the)

benefizio fatto non è mai perduto".
benefit   made   not is ever   lost

www.ingramcontent.com/pod-product-compliance
Lightning Source LLC
LaVergne TN
LVHW011326080426
835513LV00006B/220